DATE DUE

SEP 30 1999	
Oct 20 1999	
OCT 18 1999	

GAYLORD   PRINTED IN U.S.A.

Mental Health
Outcome
Evaluation

Mental Health Outcome Evaluation

DAVID C. SPEER

Louis de la Parte Florida Mental Health Institute
University of South Florida
Tampa, Florida

ACADEMIC PRESS

San Diego　　London　　Boston　　New York　　Sydney　　Tokyo　　Toronto

Copyright © 1998 by ACADEMIC PRESS

Academic Press
a division of Harcourt Brace & Company
525 B Street, Suite 1900, San Diego, California 92101-4495, USA
http://www.apnet.com

Academic Press Limited
24-28 Oval Road, London NW1 7DX, UK
http://www.hbuk.co.uk/ap/

Library of Congress Card Catalog Number: 97-80314

International Standard Book Number: 0-12-656575-9

PRINTED IN THE UNITED STATES OF AMERICA
97 98 99 00 01 02 QW 9 8 7 6 5 4 3 2 1

CONTENTS

4 What Should Be Measured? Issues

5 What Should Be Measured? Instruments

6 Potential Booby Traps and Landmines

7 Practical Implementation Issues and Suggestions

PREFACE

The 1990s have been tumultuous times for human services in general and for mental health service providers in particular. It is tempting to attribute the powerful forces assailing mental health services to political whimsy and the capriciousness of public officials and public opinion; however, almost everything in Western society reduces ultimately to economics. The effects of Reagan–Bush defense spending on the national deficit will undoubtedly be debated for years to come. The near bankruptcy of New York City and other large cities a few short years ago and the recent financial troubles of Orange County, California, brought matters closer to home. One economic dynamic has caught everyone's attention: spiraling increases in health-care costs. The current and potential effects on governmental budgets, Medicare and Medicaid, the insurance industry, business and industry, and the average citizen are well known. Cost concerns have generated questions about the associated benefits of health-care interventions; what are the likely benefits of this test, the likely results of this operation, or the likely results of this medication?

An early and enduring response to spiraling costs has been *managed care*. Health-care policy makers, governmental administrators, and corporate executives have turned *en masse* to managed care as a hoped-for panacea for seemingly out-of-control health-care costs. Mental health services, too, have been caught up in these forces. Cost-curtailment efforts have created some relatively new issues and terms for health benefits managers, managed-care administrators, and corporate benefits executives: health services outcomes, services effectiveness, and health-care outcomes. In the mental health domain, the comparable terms have been service outcomes and treatment effectiveness. These terms refer to industry efforts to assess, monitor, and capture information about the "benefits," results, and consequences of health and mental health care and treatment. Questioning the outcomes or results of treatment and care is a relatively recent phenomenon in the health-care industry. Previously, these issues concerned mainly laboratory and academic researchers and the Food and Drug Administration. Now, however, care and service delivery administrators and managers at all levels are increasingly queried about the "effectiveness" or the results of their services. Most policy, governance, and management persons, public and private alike, will have had little, if any, interest, background, or training in the research and evaluation methods involved in addressing effectiveness and service outcome issues. This book is an effort to provide such decision makers with basic concepts and methods for outcome evaluation in primary mental health-care delivery settings.

Perhaps because broad-spectrum and large-scale mental health services are relatively young in their development (being traceable only to the post-World War II years), the mental health industry finds itself poorly prepared to vigorously and cogently participate in the current debates about funding human and health-care services. Many phenomena have contributed to the relative absence of a credible mental health service knowledge base: generous government funding during the 1960s and 1970s; psychotherapy and "analysis" being faddish for a while; a breakdown in the relationship between academia and the provider community; and turf issues brought on by the biomedicalization of psychiatry and the psychosocialization of psychology, social work, and nursing.

Although there are still some who disagree, the vast majority of mental health service and psychotherapy researchers agree that mental health services "work"—at least in the laboratory. For example, for many mental health problems, a variety of forms of psychotherapy and counseling have been shown to be more effective than no treatment and various placebos, and such treatments have reasonably durable effects. Current controversies revolve around what aspects of people's problems and functioning should serve as criteria for service effectiveness, what magnitude of change qualifies as significant, how much service is necessary to achieve significant change, the lack of demonstrable differences between different kinds of service interventions, and whether or not interventions that have proven effective under highly controlled conditions in fact work in community and applied settings.

An irony of the current state of the mental health industry is that although there is voluminous research documenting service effectiveness in laboratory settings, there is relatively little information about service effectiveness in community mental health centers, clinics, and private practice offices. Information about the effects and effectiveness of mental health services in community and applied settings is desperately needed.

Consequently, researchers are currently in the throes of the development, exploration, and vigorous debate about various approaches to managed care. Managed care is a conundrum and, some would argue, has become synonymous with *cost management*. This is nowhere more apparent than in managed mental health care. However, recent interest in and concern about "continuous quality improvement" and "outcomes management" are emerging. Outcome assessment and monitoring provide an opportunity (as well as some risk) to refocus attention on the *care* aspect of managed care.

For a host of practical reasons, the research and evaluation sector of the mental health industry has, unfortunately, had great difficulty applying scientific methods in community service delivery settings. Human and health-care services *do* need a scientific knowlege base, and this has been largely provided by research in laboratory and academic settings. Until recently, funders, governing bodies, administrators, and providers have not had feasible methodological alternatives to the experimental approach. A different perspective and approach are needed to obtain effectiveness information in applied mental health settings.

The purposes of this volume are twofold. First, a different perspective or approach, an alternative to experimental methodology, will be presented. Second, outcome evaluation methods that are amenable to use in field settings will be described. This approach and these methods will probably be controversial and subject to criticism by those well grounded in the philosophy and technology of science. I hope this book will provide a bridge or link between hard science and evaluation methods and will yield useful information for decision makers in the mental health services arena.

This book is written for nonscientist decision makers and professionals: for funders, boards of directors, executives and administrators, program directors, nonscientist grant writers, and providers. It is also appropriate for "aspiring" decision makers. Those line staff providers, or clinicians in training, whose career aspirations include greater management responsibility, may be well served by learning more about outcome evaluation in applied settings. This book will also provide an alternative frame of reference for mental health services researchers who have had difficulty adapting scientific methods for feasible application in service delivery settings.

This book may also serve as a supplement or an alternative to traditional statistical method texts for graduate students in terminal master's degree programs (e.g., M.S.W., M.B.A.). Questions about the appropriateness of courses on scientific statistics for students in nonscience professional training programs have lingered for many years. Perhaps training in program evaluation would better serve students in social work and public and health administration than do courses on traditional research methods.

A few low-level statistics, such as means, standard deviations, and t and z tests are mentioned occasionally. It is assumed that the modal group of readers in positions to influence policy and program decisions will generally have at least master's degrees (e.g., M.B.A., M.P.A., M.S.W., M.S.N.). Most will have had a passing exposure to introductory statistics in their training.

I begin this book with an elaboration of why it is necessary to evaluate mental health services outcomes and then proceed to the development of an alternative framework to the traditional scientific approach. Ensuing chapters deal with the methods for determining whether or not client change has occurred, measuring relevant aspects of clients' conditions and behavior, sources of misinterpretation of data, issues surrounding significance of change, examples of outcome evaluation approaches, and implementation of data collection. Finally, I discuss whether or not outcome evaluation should be done in all settings. Because many public and private provider and managed-care entities are exploring clinician ratings as outcome information, special attention is given to this topic in Chapter 6.

A persistent tension throughout this book will be between using evaluation methods that are feasible in field settings and clinics and drawing reasonably valid conclusions. Although the uncritical application of experimental technology is challenged, evaluators still must be concerned with the principles bearing on making valid inferences and drawing conclusions from outcome evaluation information.

Examples of outcome evaluation studies among adults, children, and older adults are presented and referenced. However, the focus will be on outcome evaluation of mental health services for adults. The circumstances surrounding services for children and their families are sufficiently different and complex that a separate book on the evaluation of these services is warranted. Similarly, I do not address the measures and approaches appropriate for evaluating the outcomes of services for substance-abusing consumers.

Finally, it should be noted that outcome evaluation is *not* hassle-free. Obtaining credible information does involve doing some things differently and some inconvenience, although probably not as much as people believe. The trade-offs of some hassles and minor costs for demonstrating the worth of mental health services must be confronted.

David C. Speer

CHAPTER 1

Why Evaluate Mental Health Service Outcomes?

The current national apprehension about the spiraling costs of health care pervades almost every aspect of American society. Congress is preoccupied with the implications for the national deficit of Medicare, Medicaid, and government employees health insurance costs. State governments have similar concerns. Employers see employee health insurance costs eroding their profit margins. The insurance industry struggles to balance affordable premiums and escalating health-care costs. Health-care providers worry about whether they have done enough tests to protect themselves from malpractice litigation, and they face sky-rocketing malpractice insurance premiums. Average citizens agonize about the possible loss of health-care benefits at work, and about whether or not they could afford premium costs should such a loss of benefits occur. Deductibles and 10–20% copayments of sizable hospital and diagnostic test bills are not trivial matters for the average person.

These apprehensions have triggered increased sensitivity among governments, business and industry, insurers, and the general public about what is being obtained for the price. The likely outcomes, including risks of expensive surgery, additional medical tests, dental work, and hospital stays are being closely scrutinized. It is no surprise that similar concerns and questions are being raised about mental health services. Accountability in terms of costs and benefits has become the mantra of health-care and human services funders, providers, and consumers.

A HISTORICAL OVERVIEW, BRIEFLY

In some ways, the mental health industry has had a sheltered existence, at least until recently. It is worth remembering that psychiatry, psychotherapy, and counseling are relatively young endeavors. Although Freud began his initial inquiries into the human mind about 100 years ago, growth in broad-spectrum mental health services began only after World War II. The community mental health movement did not begin until the 1960s. Mental health rode the wave of generous governmental funding for two decades, until the effects of governmental deficit spending on out-of-control inflation were identified. During the 1960s and early 1970s, mental health was the favored child of human services growth.

The early popularity of psychoanalysis lent an aura of mystique to the mental health field. The principles of psychoanalysis were difficult for the public (and many professionals) to understand. Researchers had difficulty getting an empirical grasp on this form of treatment, and some proponents argued that the mysteries of the mind and science were mutually exclusive. In this context, and the fact that no one was vigorously demanding proof that mental health services were helpful, early efforts at accountability took the form of counting the amount of services delivered, costs, and quality assurance plans. Guidelines for appropriate services were developed by consensus, and measurement consisted primarily of counting how many clients were seen and for how many visits. The implicit consensual belief that the results of therapy really could not be measured prevailed for some time.

The first significant jolt to the fledgling mental health domain was delivered in 1952 by the British behaviorist Professor Hans Eysenck. Eysenck (1952), on the basis of his review of the research literature at that time, asserted that psychotherapy in general and psychoanalysis in particular were no more effective than the simple passage of time. His interpretation of the current research suggested that most people with anxiety and depression ("neuroses") got better eventually even without therapy. This assertion was followed by heated controversy and methodological rebuttals on both sides of the Atlantic. More significantly, Eysenck stimulated an avalanche of efficacy research among academic American psychologists and psychiatrists attempting to demonstrate that psychotherapy was in fact helpful and effective. This flurry of laboratory research continued for the next two decades.

By the mid-1980s, a consensus was emerging among academic researchers that psychotherapy and a variety of psychosocial interventions had been proven to be effective under controlled conditions (e.g., Garfield & Bergin, 1986; Lambert, 1991; Lambert & Bergin, 1994; Lipsey & Wilson, 1993; Smith, Glass, & Miller, 1980). Although there continued to be detractors (e.g., Albee, 1990; Jacobson, 1995), Lambert concluded, among other things, that psychotherapy is effective, it is more effective than placebo interventions, and that clients who improve maintain that improvement for extended periods (Lambert, 1991; Lambert & Bergin, 1994). Lipsey and Wilson (1993) reported that psychological and behavioral interventions are as effective for mental health problems as most medical interventions are for medical illnesses, and more effective than many medical procedures for medical conditions.

CURRENT ISSUES

In the recent heated debates about the costs of health care, including mental health care, outpatient psychotherapy has been proposed as a cost-effective alternative to expensive inpatient care for many mental illness conditions (e.g., Pallak & Cummings, 1994). However, third-party payers and managed care organizations are strenuously resisting reimbursement for ambulatory mental health care at rates comparable to reimbursement for care for medical illnesses (the parity issue). There are a number of reasons for this.

The profit motive and conflicts of interest undoubtedly play a role among private-sector managed care entities. However, Lambert (1991), among others, has connected reimbursement for services with service outcomes:

> Psychotherapy and psychotherapy research take place in a financial and political climate of accountability. Without demonstrable outcomes it seems unlikely that psychotherapy can continue to be covered by national or independent health care systems. The mounting pressure to find fast, effective, permanent cures is great. (p. 2)

This intense concern about service and program outcomes is pervading all funding sources, public and private, including grant-making foundations. In the current environment of shrinking resources, service agencies such as family service associations are increasingly turning to alternative funding sources. However, governmental agencies and foundations that previously funded demonstration programs are now requiring outcome evaluation plans as part of the grant application process.

But what about the volumes of research indicating that psychotherapy and counseling are efficacious? Beutler and Clarkin (1991) expressed the view that psychotherapy research findings have low "believability." There continues to be an aura of mystery surrounding mental health services. This is akin to the "black box" phenomenon; we know it works but we can't explain why it works. Researchers have contributed to the problem by not communicating their findings to the public and by reporting findings in ways that are difficult for funding sources, policy makers, and providers to comprehend (e.g., effect sizes, percent of treated clients better than average control client) (Speer, 1994).

Recently, Goldfried and Wolfe (1996) and Newman and Tejeda (1996), too, have taken the scientific mental health community to task for its failed responsibility for communicating effectively with stakeholders, including practitioners.

Another source of skepticism is the repeated finding that diverse kinds of psychosocial interventions seem to have equivalent effects and for varying kinds of mental health problems. Beutler and Clarkin (1991) have commented that this counterintuitive state of affairs fuels doubts among third-party payers. Garfield and Bergin (1986), too, have expressed the view that this lack of intervention definitiveness has raised skepticism about all interventions among reimbursement executives and political leaders.

A recently emerging concern, and an issue central to the focus of this book, is that mental health service and psychotherapy efficacy findings under laboratory and controlled conditions have generally not been duplicated in field or community service settings (e.g., Coyle, 1996). This is the *external validity* problem of experimental laboratory research; that is, because something can be proven to work in the lab does not necessarily mean that it will work outside the lab. Weisz, Weiss, and Donenberg (1992) and Seligman (1995) have articulated the numerous dimensions upon which laboratory psychotherapy settings and procedures differ from those in community mental health clinics and other applied settings. Weisz and colleagues (1992) expressed the view that the effectiveness of psychotherapy and counseling for children and adolescents in community and field settings had not been established in the early 1990s. Recently, Weisz, Donenberg, Weiss, and Han (1995) reported that the few available studies of the effectiveness of therapy for children in field settings show markedly poorer outcomes than laboratory studies of psychotherapy. Given the dearth of efforts to evaluate the effectiveness of community-based mental health services in general, the same questions might be raised about services for adults as well (Speer, 1994; Speer & Newman, 1996).

The problem is not that community-based services have been shown to be ineffective. The problem is that until recently there has been little effort to even examine the question, with one exception—for a brief period in the mid-1970s. The National Institute of Mental Health (NIMH) mandated that community mental health centers that received federal funds had to evaluate the effects of their services. However, with the advent of deregulation, this initiative rapidly dissipated. The relative absence of information documenting the effects of community-based mental health services has fueled skepticism among third-party payers, policy makers, and the public.

Federal research funding sources, too, have acknowledged the distinction between the effectiveness of psychosocial interventions under controlled laboratory conditions and the effectiveness of psychosocial interventions as usually practiced in community settings. The term *efficacy* has been used to refer to the former, and the term *effectiveness* research to the latter (NIMH, 1990). A similar distinction has been drawn between "clinical research" and "clinical services research" (Attkisson et al., 1992; NIMH, 1991). Although for research funding purposes considerable scientific rigor is still required for effectiveness and services research, these distinctions underscore the growing concern about and importance of obtaining information about how mental health interventions work in the field.

Other issues, largely ignored by the mental health industry, have contributed to public puzzlement about what is being obtained for the cost. For example, it has been known for some time now that in public outpatient mental health clinics 50% of clients receive four or fewer counseling or psychotherapy sessions; 25% do not return after their first visit. It is also well documented that about 50% of outpatients drop out of treatment without informing or discussing their decisions with their therapists (Phillips, 1991). These facts raise nagging questions about the appropriateness and acceptability of traditional outpatient services for a large proportion of the help-seeking public. Pekarik's (1992) finding that outpatients who discontinue treatment early are more troubled than those who continue receiving services for longer periods lends a sobering tone to the outpatient services landscape. This may provide support to some payers who believe that mental health outpatients really do not have serious problems (that they are "the worried well"). Although noncompliance with medical treatment and recommendations is a common phenomenon, noncompliance with mental health service recommendations has largely been ignored.

Third-party payers and managed care entities have made great use of selected findings from Howard's and colleagues study of the relationship between length of treatment and treatment outcomes (Howard, Kopta, Krause, & Orlinsky, 1986). This is the seminal mental health "dose-response" research in which it was found that there is, for the most part, a direct relationship between the amount of outpatient treatment and the amount of client improvement. The parts of the findings that third-party payers took most seriously were that half of outpatients are improved after eight psychotherapy sessions, and that 75% are improved after 26 sessions. Managed care does not yet seem to have taken note of Kopta, Howard, Lowry, and Beutler's (1994) finding that the typical outpatient requires about 1 year of treatment to have an 85% chance of symptomatic recovery.

On the other hand, the credibility of the effectiveness of community-based mental health services recently received a significant boost from a survey of over 4000 readers of *Consumer Reports* (Fowler, 1995; "Mental Health: Does Therapy Help?", 1995; Seligman, 1995). The majority who responded to the survey were highly satisfied with the care they received, most reported having made significant strides toward resolving the problems that led to treatment, and almost all said life had become more manageable. Although there are questions about the methodological soundness of the survey (e.g., Hollon, 1996; Jacobson & Christensen, 1996; also, see Chapters 3 and 5), these findings from an independent consumer advocate group provide a significant increment of potential credibility to the public.

The point here is that Howard and his colleagues are among the few researchers of note who have attempted to study the effectiveness of outpatient mental health services "in the field" or in applied settings. There is a slowly growing body of outcome research focusing on community support services, residential treatment, and case management for adults with severe and persistent mental illness in the community (Speer & Newman, 1996). The problem is that there is too little outcome research being done in community service delivery settings. Scattered findings from a few studies can be easily dismissed as unreplicated by those with vested interests in keeping reimbursement rates for mental health services low. Indicative of the problem were the findings from a recent computerized literature search on mental health services effectiveness research for the years 1989 through 1995. Over 500 titles were located; however, closer examination of the reports indicated that only 39 were, in fact, databased outcome evaluation studies (Speer & Newman, 1996). A lot is being said, but little is being done. Mental health providers and service organizations would do themselves a lot of good in the long run by supporting, or perhaps encouraging, outcome and effectiveness research in their settings.

Indicative of the urgency surrounding these issues was the 1995 American Psychological Association Annual Convention in New York. Although psychologists, along with the other mental health professionals, have been paying increasing attention to outcome evaluation in recent years, this meeting was characterized by an unusually large number of presentations, panels, and symposia on outcome evaluation. Many speakers reported that third-party payers were beginning to demand treatment outcome information and documentation that consumers of mental health services are able to function adequately, for example, in their work settings. One speaker cited by Cavaliere (1995) asserted that practitioners who balk at the extra time and paperwork involved in outcome tracking may find themselves unable to obtain or keep positions on provider panels. John Weisz (cited by Cavaliere, 1995) reiterated that outcome researchers should conduct more studies in clinics and in private practices rather than just in controlled laboratory settings.

In this context, it was discouraging in 1996 to hear representatives of large private-sector corporations still discussing their monitoring of contracted mental health benefits for their employess (e.g., employee assistance programs) largely in quality assurance and utilization review terms. Although these dimensions of mental health service management are definitely important, mental health service purchasers and providers have hidden accountability behind quality assurance for decades with little effort invested in determining the outcomes of their services. This is akin to monitoring surgery to make sure that it was done properly but neglecting to inquire about the patients' conditions a week later. It is good to know that the surgery was successful, but whether or not the patient survived is also pertinent.

MANAGED MENTAL HEALTH CARE

There is little disagreement that managed care, in some form, is here to stay for the foreseeable future. Although hope abounds that managed care will be able to significantly rein in escalating health-care costs, considerable debate and angst is occurring about the eventual form of viable and efficient managed care. "Managed care" is considered by some to be a euphemism for utilization management or cost management. There are lingering questions about whether or not managed care has been able to significantly reduce costs (Knight, 1996; Sederer & Bennett, 1996). Concerns about the quality of care being provided to the poor and the elderly are beginning to emerge. There are concerns about private managed care entities shifting costs to the public sector by discharging or refusing to enroll high users of health-care services, such as the elderly during their last year of life.

Things are even more unclear in the mental health domain. Experience with mental health and psychiatric services in health maintenance organizations (HMOs; "carved-in" mental health services) suggest that these services are viewed largely as a mechanism for reducing *medical* care utilization and costs, rather than being viewed as legitimate health services in their own right. Mental health services in managed care settings are often victims of the general discouragement of use of specialist services as a cost-containment mechanism. Coyle (1996) has recently suggested that the focus on utilization and cost containment, to the exclusion of quality and outcome considerations, is moving managed mental health care dangerously close to "mismanagement." A recent request for proposals for a Medicaid Behavioral Health Care Utilization Management service in one state only alluded to outcome evaluation in passing. Suspicion is also arising that case management, in some proprietary organizations, too, is being converted into a utilization and cost management tool rather than being a consumer advocacy service. It is as yet unclear where the loci for services for the severely and persistently mentally ill will reside; care and treatment of these vulnerable people are often expensive, making them fiscally unattractive to proprietary managed care groups.

As of this writing, a few large managed care organization have been developing "first-generation" outcome monitoring and evaluation systems. Many of these systems are based on provider ratings; more will be said about provider rating assessments later (Chapter 6). One system, the COMPASS Treatment System, described by Sperry, Brill, Howard, and Grisson (1996), uses both provider and consumer self-administering assessment methods. This group has done a considerable amount of development, validity, and demonstration work in outpatient sevice settings; work in inpatient and substance abuse treatment settings is in progress. However, outcome evaluation in managed care does not yet appear to have evolved on a broad scale basis.

In a recent review of managed mental health care, Sederer and Bennett (1996) discussed a variety of issues such as what conditions are to be insured, mental health services provided within primary care settings in HMOs ("carve-ins"), mental health services provided separately from or outside primary care setting in HMOs ("carve-outs"), types of provider networks, contracting and liability, and ethics and conflicts of interest. Service outcomes and effectiveness of services were alluded to as potential criteria to aid in managed care decision making. There was a sense, however, that assessment of service outcomes in managed mental health care is a somewhat uncertain and vague enterprise. There is also lingering concern that the evolution of technology for service outcome assessment is lagging behind that of the technology for assessment of financial and other organizational matters. Part of the dilemma here is that evaluators and researchers lack adequate experience in the field testing of methods for assessing service outcomes in community settings.

Cuffel, Snowden, Lasland, and Piccagli (1993) pointed out that the contractual relationships between payers, providers, and consumers in managed mental health care have historically been fallible because any one party could act in its own best interests to the detriment of another party. This problem can occur in mental health when providers cannot be held accountable because their practices or the outcomes of their services are unknown. Sederer and Bennett (1996) predicted that the narrow focus on cost containment is likely to wane or to be incorporated into outcome-oriented management.

It has been suggested that equitable reimbursement for ambulatory mental health services (parity) may hinge on increased documentation of the positive consequences of community-based mental health services. Outcome evaluation technology is evolving. Funding sources are showing significant interest in, if not demanding, outcome or effectiveness information. The next step that requires increased attention is determining *how* outcome information is to be used in service delivery and clinical management. Terms such as *continuous quality improvement, culture of measurement,* and *outcomes management* are increasingly appearing in the mental health outcome evaluation literature. These terms all refer to the internal service provider administrative and management processes whereby outcome information is used to enhance the effectiveness of services. Sperry and his colleagues (1996) provided some examples of outcome information being used to monitor consumer progress, as feedback for clinical providers, as input for quality assurance reviews, and potentially to assist in better matching of providers with specific consumer clinical needs.

As of this writing, managed mental health care appears on the verge of being dominated by cost-containment values. It is possible that public outcries may help restore a balancing of cost considerations with a greater focus on the quality and effectiveness of services. The mental health field has gotten a late start in evaluating the effectiveness of services, but strides are being made in refocusing the field on consumer *care*. Mental health service delivery organizations can aid this process by getting more actively involved in trying out, piloting, testing, and developing methods and systems for assessing outcomes and evaluating the effectiveness of their services. There are many unanswered questions and much needs to be done, but the mental health field can enhance the care provided to consumers by focusing greater attention on the consequences and results of the services it provides.

REFERENCES

Albee, G. W. (1990). The futility of psychotherapy. *The Journal of Mind and Body, 11,* 369–384.

Attkisson, C., Cook, J., Karno, M., Lehman, A., McGlashan, T. H., Melzer, H. Y., O'Connor, M., Richardson, D., Bosenblatt, A., Wells, K., Williams, J., & Hohman, A. A. (1992). Clinical services research. *Schizophrenia Bulletin, 18,* 389–406.

Beutler, L. E., & Clarkin, J. (1991). Future research directions. In L. E. Beutler & M. Crago (Eds.), *Psychotherapy research: An international review of programmatic studies* (pp. 329–334). Washington, DC: American Psychological Association.

Cavaliere, F. (1995). Payers demand increased provider documentation. *The APA Monitor, 26,* (10), 41.

Coyle, J. T. (1996). Foreword. In L. I. Sederer & B. Dickey (Eds.), *Outcomes assessment in clinical practice* (pp. v–vii). Baltimore: Williams & Wilkins.

Cuffel, B. J., Snowden, L., Masland, M., & Piccagli, G. (1993). Managed care in the public mental health system. *Community Mental Health Journal, 32,* 109–124.

Eysenck, H. J. (1952). The effects of psychotherapy: An evaluation. *Journal of Consulting Psychology, 16,* 319–324.

Fowler, R. D. (1995). Survey results show psychotherapy works. *The APA Monitor, 26,* (12), 3.

Garfield, S. L. & Bergin, A. E. (Eds.). (1986). *Handbook of psychotherapy and behavior change* (3rd ed.). New York: Wiley.

Goldfried, M. R., & Wolfe, B. E. (1996). Psychotherapy practice and research: Repairing a strained alliance. *American Psychologist, 51,* 1007–1016.

Hollon, S. D. (1996). The efficacy and effectiveness of psychotherapy relative to medications. *American Psychologist, 51,* 1025–1030.

Howard, K. I., Kopta, S. M., Krause, M. S., & Orlinsky, D. E. (1986). The dose-effect relationship in psychotherapy. *American Psychologist, 41,* 159–164.

Jacobson, N. (1995, March–April). The overselling of therapy. *The Family Therapy Networker,* 41–47.

Jacobson, N. S., & Christensen, A. (1996). Studying the effectiveness of psychotherapy: How well can clinical trials do the job? *American Psychologist, 51,* 1031–1039.

Knight, B. (1996). *Managed care and the future of mental health and aging.* Keynote address, Representatives of State Mental Health Programs for Older Persons Annual Conference. Austin, Texas.

Kopta, S. M., Howard, K. I., Lowry, J. L., & Beutler, L. E. (1994). Patterns of symptomatic recovery in psychotherapy. *Journal of Consulting and Clinical Psychology, 62,* 1009–1016.

Lambert, M. J. (1991). Introduction to psychotherapy research. In L. E. Beutler & M. Crago (Eds.), *Psychotherapy research: An international review of programmatic studies* (pp. 1–12). Washington, DC: American Psychological Association.

Lambert, M. J., & Bergin, A. E. (1994). The effectiveness of psychotherapy. In A. E. Bergin & S. L. Garfield (Eds.), *Handbook of psychotherapy and behavior change* (4th ed., pp. 143–189). New York: Wiley.

Lipsey, M. W., & Wilson, D. B. (1993). The efficacy of psychological, educational, and behavioral treatment: Confirmation from meta-analysis. *American Psychologist, 48,* 1181–1209.

Mental health: Does therapy help? (1995, November). *Consumer Reports, 60,* (11), 734–739.

National Institute of Mental Health. (1990). *Program announcement: Research on effectiveness and outcomes of mental health services.* Rockville, MD: Department of Health and Human Services.

National Institute of Mental Health. (1991). *Caring for people with severe mental disorders: A national plan of research to improve services.* Washington, DC: Superintendent of Documents. (U.S. Government Printing Office, DHHS Publication No. (ADM) 91–1762).

Newman, F. L., & Tejeda, M. J. (1996). The need for research that is designed to support decisions in the delivery of mental health services. *American Psychologist, 51,* 1040–1049.

Pallak, M. S., & Cummings, N. A. (1994). Outcome research in managed beehavioral health care: Issues, strategies, and trends. In S. A. Shueman, W. G. Troy, & S. L. Mayhugh (Eds.), *Managed behavioral health care* (pp. 205–221). Springfield, IL: Thomas.

Pekarik, G. (1992). Posttreatment adjustment of clients who drop out early vs. late in treatment. *Journal of Clinical Psychology, 48,* 379–387.

Phillips, E. L. (1991). George Washington University's international data on psychotherapy delivery systems: Modeling new approaches to the study of therapy. In L. E. Beutler & M. Crago (Eds.), *Psychotherapy research: An international review of programmatic studies* (pp. 263–273). Washington, DC: American Psychological Association.

Seligman, M. F. (1995). The effectiveness of psychotherapy: The Consumer Reports Study. *American Psychologist, 50,* 965–974.

Sederer, L. I., & Bennett, M. J. (1996). Managed mental health care in the United States: A status report. *Administration and Policy in Mental Health, 23,* 289–306.

Smith, M. L., Glass, G. V., & Miller, T. L. (1980). *The benefits of psychotherapy.* Baltimore: The Johns Hopkins University Press.

Speer, D.C. (1994). Can treatment research inform decision makers? Nonexperimental method issues and examples among older outpatients. *Journal of Consulting and Clinical Psychology, 62,* 560–568.

Speer, D. C., & Newman, F. L. (1996). Mental health services outcome evaluation. *Clinical Psychology: Science and Practice, 3,* 105–129.

Sperry, L., Brill, P. L., Howard, K. I., & Grissom, G. R. (1996). *Treatment outcomes in psychotherapy and psychiatric interventions.* New York: Brunner/Mazel.

Weisz, J. R., Donenberg, G. R., Weiss, B., & Han, S. S. (1995). Bridging the gap between laboratory and clinic in child and adolescent psychotherapy. *Journal of Consulting and Clinical Psychology, 63,* 688–701.

Weisz, J. R., Weiss, B., & Donenberg, G. R. (1992). The lab versus the clinic: Effects of child and adolescent psychotherapy. *American Psychologist, 47,* 1578–1585.

CHAPTER 2

A Different Perspective: Practical Outcome Evaluation

Outcomes and evaluation need to be defined. By *outcomes* I mean the assessment of any characteristics of consumers' behavior, condition, or adjustment that are significantly related to the reason for seeking mental health services. This assessment occurs during or after service receipt. In later chapters on measurement (Chapters 4 and 5), more will be said about single and multiple dimensions of clients' adjustment, whose point of view is chosen, and the significance of the dimensions. By *evaluation* I mean the systematic examination of such assessment during and/or consequent to the service. With Suchman (1967) and Cronbach and his colleagues (1980), I believe the purpose of evaluation is to inform or "enlighten" deliberations about the value, worth, significance, and/or future form of services, rather than providing new knowledge, proving cause-and-effect relationships, or producing conclusive facts. From the standpoint of concern about external validity (e.g., "Does it work outside of the laboratory?"), practical outcome evaluation is viewed as approximate replication in applied settings of what has been demonstrated in controlled settings. Generally speaking, the primary focus is *not* producing new knowledge. The target audience is primarily policy decision makers, funding and reimbursement executives, and service managers rather than the scientific community.

It is assumed that the comprehension and utilization of a body of evidence about the effectiveness or outcomes of mental health services will occur within a complex context of multiple perspectives, stakeholders, and interests. These include Congress, federal agencies, state program directors and legislatures, third-party payers, managed care entities, the various constituents of the health-care industry, agency boards of directors and executives, service program directors and providers, and public perceptions of the nature of mental health services and their benefits. As Cronbach et al. (1980), among others, pointed out, policy, funding, and reimbursement decision making are usually not rational processes and may or may not be influenced by objective information. There are myriad forces influencing public decision making, including attitudes, fads, biases, vested interests, political agendas, perceptions of resources, special interests, and economic considerations. The task of the mental health industry is to provide comprehensible and credible mental health service effectiveness information for this mix of competing and conflicting interests.

Early efforts to apply scientific methodology to mental health program evaluation were characterized by application of laboratory and experimental approaches. These very soon proved not to be feasible on a variety of ethical and practical service delivery grounds. Service providers rebelled against the idea of random assignment. Vigorous debates between leading methodologists about the appropriateness of the experimental approach was followed by a near paralysis of systematic efforts to investigate service outcomes and effectiveness in community service settings.

As I shall demonstrate shortly, the place of scientific methodology in practical program evaluation is not a simple, all-or-none matter. The dilemma has been that scientists have been inordinately critical of empirical methods that are feasible in applied settings, and community provider organizations have allowed themselves to be intimidated into near immobility by this criticism. The attitude that if evaluation cannot be done "scientifically" than it should not be done at all seems to have prevailed. The consequence is that the much needed service outcome evaluation has simply not been done to a degree that would gain the attention of the significant actors in the political arena governing mental health service programs.

Among the seven leading program evaluation proponents discussed by Shadish, Cook, and Leviton (1991), the functional or pragmatic accommodation perspective of Professor Lee J. Cronbach seems the most useful in providing the field with a viable basis for pursuing practical outcome evaluation (Cronbach, 1982; Cronbach et al., 1980). It should be kept in mind that program evaluation has its roots in the scientific approach, and that the leading thinkers in the area were scientists first. Professor Cronbach, one of the preeminent social scientists and methodologists of this century, has been one of the more practical critics of exclusive application of scientifically rigorous methodology and experimental design to providing useful evaluative information for decision makers. Although few disagree that the experimental approach (i.e., randomly assigning research participants to different treatments) potentially provides relatively more "certain" and definitive findings, this approach has important economic and informational costs when applied in the public information domain.

The basic issues reduce to two matters: conclusiveness versus uncertainty and external validity (other settings to which findings may be generalized). Randomized experimentation is driven by (a) primary concern with conclusively demonstrating that it is the intervention that produces the change (i.e., proving cause and effect) and (b) rendering as implausible as possible other explanations of the change (i.e., rival hypotheses) (e.g., Kazdin, 1994). Thus the standard in psychotherapy efficacy studies or clinical trials is (a) standardized treatment protocols or manuals for implementation of the intervention, (b) for fixed numbers of sessions, (c) applied by clinicians highly trained in the specific intervention, (d) independent or external monitoring of clinician adherence to the protocol, and (e) treatment of clearly specified and homogeneous clients (f) randomly assigned to the intervention and comparison conditions.

Cronbach (1980) argues that the priority given to proving that it is the intervention, and only the specified intervention, that causes the change, is misplaced. He argues that this certainty is purchased at the cost of being able to generalize the results to other settings (i.e., applied settings), the representativeness of the conditions under which services are provided in the field, and relevance. Recently, Goldfried and Wolfe (1996) pointed out that efficacy studies and clinical trials are the wrong methods for evaluating the effectiveness of mental health services as they are actually provided under real life clinical conditions. Cronbach argues that threats to drawing valid conclusions are always present, even in highly controlled experimental studies, and that stringent efforts to control potentially confounding variables often create such artificial conditions that the evaluator is no longer testing the intervention under normal operating conditions. Trivial issues are often studied well. External validity, or generalizing results to community service settings, is limited because the implementation procedures are rarely feasible outside of experimental or laboratory settings (see Weisz et al., 1992, and Seligman, 1995). Cronbach applies the concept of *validity*, or plausibility, to the rational process of drawing conclusions, rather than to methods and studies, per se.

Cronbach has argued that not only is randomized experimentation economically costly and often ethically not possible within many service delivery settings, it often detracts from addressing important public questions and produces a limited range of information that is of limited use to decision makers. Randomized experimentation should be considered as only one approach in the methodological armamentarium of program evaluators. He proposes that program evaluators, although guided by the most rigorous methodology possible in the community service setting circumstances, accept the trade-off of increased "uncertainty" or the possibility of confounding influences for greater relevance and applicability in service delivery settings. Evidence for the validity of conclusions can accumulate through replication of results in other community settings; replication of laboratory methods in the community is unlikely. Cronbach et al. (1980), and Campbell and Stanley (1963) have expressed the view that rival or competing explanations for findings should be "plausible" and cogent (not just theoretically possible) in order to be taken as serious alternatives to the conclusion that services in the community are effective.

Cronbach is methodologically pluralistic and has suggested, for example, that intake or admission assessments (baseline) may be suitable comparison conditions in many circumstances. Similarly, for large programs in operation for a long time, he proposes descriptive, longitudinal, single-group methods for study of program outcomes (Cronbach, 1982; Cronbach et al., 1980; Shadish et al., 1991). More will be said about this in the next chapter. Cronbach believes that evaluation's greatest value is providing input or feedback in the processes of deliberation and decision making about the forms, modifications, and characteristics of services over time (formative evaluation). He also believes that the goal of evaluation as an ultimate or final judge of the absolute effectiveness, value, or worth of services (summative evaluation) is usually unrealistic and inappropriate given the multiplicity of factors influencing public policy formation, service funding, service delivery, and consumers' responses to service.

Sperry, Brill, Howard, and Grissom (1996), too, have recently challenged the role of the experimental method or randomized clinical trials in practical outcome evaluation. These authors recommended a "quasi-naturalistic" approach that systematically uses exploratory methodology. They too suggest that greater emphasis be placed on the generalizability of findings to other service delivery settings and the use of replication of results in other similar service settings to support valid conclusions of treatment effectiveness.

Now, having challenged the primacy of the rigid scientific approach in mental health services outcome evaluation, we need to back up and consider some aspects of scientific reasoning and methods. What has been questioned above is largely the slavish devotion to the randomized experimental model in evaluating the effectiveness of mental health services. In the broad domain of scientific thinking and methodology, there are other issues that need to be considered; there is significant overlap in the domains of science and program evaluation. Even though we are *not* prescribing laboratory experimentation in community service delivery settings, we do need to be concerned about matters that influence drawing reasonably defensible conclusions.

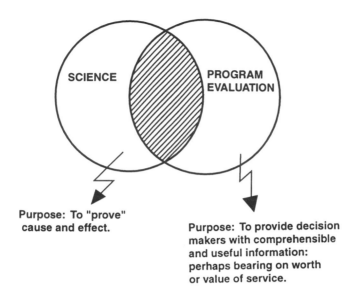

FIGURE 1   The relationship between program evaluation and science.

The relationship between science and program evaluation is represented in Figure 1. One of the primary goals of science is to prove that something *causes* something else and in such a way as to be able to convincingly rule out other explanations. The goal of program evaluation, on the other hand, is to provide decision makers with comprehensible and useful information about services; albeit, information that may be less conclusive and definitive than that provided by laboratory experiments. We are trading some degree of certainty for added relevance and, hopefully, use.

As Figure 1 suggests there is overlap, and this overlap has to do with attempting to reduce uncertainty as much as is realistically possible. Specifically, we do need to be concerned with valid and reliable measuring instruments administered in such a way as to minimize pressures to respond in artificial ways. An example might be use of a validated, self-administering questionnaire to obtain clients' reports of their depression rather than having therapists, who have a vested interest in program effectiveness, rate clients' depression (more on this matter in Chapter 6). Another example is providing clients with a questionnaire on which they can anonymously report their satisfaction with the services they received rather than having therapists interview their clients about clients' satisfaction with the treatment they have received; it is awkward and intimidating to consider telling a presumed expert, face to face, that he or she is insensitive, that he or she does not seemed to have understood one's problem, or that being kept waiting 15 minutes for an appointment is rude.

Another matter that science and program evaluation have in common is that drawing conclusions is often facilitated by being able to compare people's behavior with some other behavior. This "other behavior" may be that of a different group of people, people's own behavior at a different point in time, or people who provided the norms for standardizing a questionnaire or measurement instrument.

A recent small-scale outcome evaluation, of arguable "scientific" purity, of a supported housing project for 20 persistently and severely mentally ill older adults provides further examples (O'Sullivan & Speer, 1995). One of the issues of interest to the funders and the staff was client quality of life. To address this in part, a previously validated self-administering depression questionnaire for older adults but without general public norms was administered to the clients on several occasions. Random assignment of clients to different housing arrangements was not an option. In a previous study, the same instrument had been used to assess the mood over several occasions of a group of Parkinson's disease patients and their caregivers. The supported housing program clients and the Parkinson's disease patients and caregivers were approximately the same age. Although the data were collected at widely different times, and the life problems of the people were very different, the Parkinson's disease groups did provide a reference point for considering the self-reported depression data of the supported housing clients. Some kind of a comparison group or reference point is better than a no-comparison condition. This is an example of the nonequivalent comparison group approach of quasi-experimental research design that will be discussed further in the next chapter.

The example of use of Parkinson's disease patients and caregivers as comparison groups for a mental health outcome study reminds us that there is a need for creativity and imagination in the broader domain of outcome evaluation. Scientists are giving increasing attention to the "transportability" of laboratory treatment findings into field settings and clinics. We must not allow ourselves to be locked into traditional modals and approaches to the exclusion of other possibilities. For example, Clarke (1995) recently proposed including samples of both highly selected, homogeneous consumers without comorbid conditions *and* relatively unselected heterogeneous consumers with comorbid conditions in the same evaluation studies. Such a strategy would allow investigation of theoretical treatment issues while simultaneously moving toward generalizability of findings from consumers more like those seen in applied community settings. In a somewhat different vein, Newman and Tejeda (1996) proposed that rather than study what effects fixed amounts of services have on consumers, evaluators should specify what levels of distress and functioning should be achieved by treatment and then investigate how much and what kind of service is required to obtain the specified levels of outcome.

Finally, a point of clarification. The scientific approach and laboratory efficacy studies of mental health interventions have been challenged above on the grounds that their methods are difficult, if not impossible, to apply and replicate in community and applied settings. This should not be taken to mean that this research and the findings are of little worth or value. Laboratory studies have provided the scientific knowledge base for community-based services; we would indeed be on thin ice without them. The issue is the transferability of the laboratory results, what I have called their external validity. The relationship between laboratory studies of mental health intervention efficacy and evaluation of services effectiveness in applied settings is analogous to the relationship between chemists and chemical engineers. It is one thing for chemists, under sterile laboratory conditions, to create a new and potentially useful compound; it is another matter for the engineers to be able to develop the equipment and methods to viably produce the compound in large volume and in such a way as to be economically profitable in the marketplace. Some discoveries and inventions can be proven to be feasible outside of the laboratory and some cannot. However, the engineers do need the chemists to provide the starting points, guidance, and direction. Perhaps, service administrators and program evaluators can be viewed as the engineers of the mental health industry.

REFERENCES

Campbell, D. T., & Stanley, J. C. (1963). *Experimental and quasi-experimental designs for research.* Chicago: Rand McNally.

Clarke, G. N. (1995). Improving the transition from basic efficacy research to effectiveness studies: Methodological issues and procedures. *Journal of Consulting and Clinical Psychology, 63,* 718–725.

Cronbach, L. J. (1982). *Designing evaluations of educational and social programs.* San Francisco: Jossey-Bass.

Cronbach, L. J., Ambron, S. R., Dornbush, S. M., Hess, R. D., Hornik, R. C., Phillips, D. C., Walker, D. F., & Weiner, S. S. (1980). *Toward reform of program evaluation.* San Francisco: Jossey-Bass.

Goldfried, M. R., & Wolfe, B. E. (1996). Psychotherapy practice and research: Repairing a strained alliance. *American Psychologist, 51,* 1007–1016.

Kazdin, A. E. (1994). Methodology, design, and evaluation in psychotherapy research. In A. E. Bergin & S. L. Garfield (Eds.), *Handbook of psychotherapy and behavior change* (4th ed., pp. 19–71). New York: Wiley.

Newman, F. L., & Tejeda, M. J. (1996). The need for research that is designed to support decisions in the delivery of mental health services. *American Psychologist, 51,* 1040–1049.

O'Sullivan, M., & Speer, D. C. (1995). *The supported housing program, Broward County elderly services, Ft. Lauderdale, Florida: Evaluation final report.* Tampa, FL: Florida Mental Health Institute.

Seligman, M. F. (1995). The effectiveness of psychotherapy: The *Consumer Reports* study. *American Psychologist, 50,* 965–974.

Shadish, W. R., Cook, T. D., & Leviton, L. C. (1991). *Foundations of program evaluation: Theories of practice.* Newbury Park, CA: Sage.

Sperry, L., Brill, P. L., Howard, K. I., & Grisson, G. R. (1996). *Treatment outcomes in psychotherapy and psychiatric interventions.* New York: Brunner/Mazel.

Suchman, E. A. (1967). *Evaluative research.* New York: Russell Sage Foundation.

Weisz, J. R., Weiss, B., & Donenberg, G. R. (1992). The lab versus the clinic: Effects of child and adolescent psychotherapy. *American Psychologist, 47,* 1578–1585.

CHAPTER 3

So, How Do We Tell If Something Works?

The evaluation of the outcomes of mental health services is in most instances concerned with documenting change or benefit. In order to assess change or differentness, some kind of comparison is required. This Chapter is about determining what kinds of comparisons are feasible in a given service setting, and the planning of the evaluation logistics so that the comparisons can be made after the outcome information has been collected.

In most acute care and ambulatory care settings, we usually focus on positive change or improvement; in other words, after receiving services clients are more like average people in the general population than like consumers just beginning treatment. In programs providing services to persistently and severely mentally ill persons, on the other hand, evaluators may be less concerned with demonstrating improvement than with documenting the absence of deterioration or exacerbation of symptoms. Knapp and colleagues' (1994) evaluation of the adjustment and quality of life of 40 elderly state hospital patients 9 months after moving into a community residence and support services program, relative to their adjustment while in the hospital, is an example. The lack of significant changes in measures of morale, depression, and social activities were interpreted to indicate that these vulnerable clients had not deteriorated in the community.

There are service programs, particularly those serving populations with severe and chronic problems, in which both positive change and lack of change, and/or negative change, are found. This kind of situation is usually the richest in implications for redesigning or modifying programs and services, and for reconsidering policies. An example is the outcome evaluation of an intensive family and school-based treatment program for 19 severely maladjusted children and youth conducted by Clarke, Schaefer, Burchard, and Welkowitz (1992). They found that although the program was very effective in modifying the behavior of the young people at home, their adjustment in the school setting did not improve significantly. The bottom line, however, is that ideally evaluators want to know whether or not the consumers are different than when they began receiving services, or whether they are different than or similar to some other group of people. Ideally, one would like to be able to evaluate change on the basis of having assessed clients on at least two different occasions, one near the beginning of service and one toward the end of receiving service.

SAMPLES AND COHORTS

In scientific research, the ideal situation is that subjects are randomly selected from the larger population so that the findings from the experiment can be generalized or extrapolated to that larger population (to people not included in the study); thus, the term "sampling".[1] In outcome evaluation work, on the other hand, clients or consumers are usually not randomly selected for a variety of practical and feasibility reasons. Instead, groups of clients are chosen to be included in some other systematic way, such as all clients admitted to a program during a specified time period (e.g., a 3-month period). An admission *cohort* is every individual admitted to service during a particular interval of time. The term *sample* implies random selection. To avoid confusion we will, and the reader is encouraged to, use the term *cohort* unless the persons participating in the evaluation have in fact been randomly chosen.

That the cohort is "representative of" or like other clients, and thus findings from the cohort can be generalized to other clients in the same or other settings, can be determined in at least two ways. First, by comparing the admission clinical and sociodemographic characteristics of the cohort with those of other clients seen in the same setting, it can be determined whether or not the cohort clients are like other clients. Second, the change findings from the cohort can be compared to those of another cohort from a prior or subsequent time period and their similarity can be evaluated. Representativeness can thus be demonstrated by replication.

[1]Professor Ken Howard (personal communication, February 1997) has pointed out that this "ideal" situation is, in reality, a logical impossibility. The populations to which we wish to generalize are always in the *future* and thus cannot be truly sampled.

EVALUATION COMPARISONS

The selection of groups of consumers and groups of other people with whom they will be compared, along with planning the number and timing of assessments, are issues that technically fall in the domain of research or evaluation *design*. Once these decisions are made, it is assumed that they will be adhered to throughout the period of the evaluation study. Changing the characteristics of groups, the service or intervention, or the timing of assessments midway through the evaluation period can seriously complicate interpretion or understanding of the results at the end of the period.

The epitome of scientific research comparisons is the Experimental or Randomized Control Group Design (Campbell & Stanley, 1963); in medicine and psychiatry this is referred to as the randomized clinical trial. Here the experimental intervention and the clients to receive the intervention are carefully specified, and the clients are then randomly split into two groups, one that receives the intervention and one that does not. Ideally, both groups are assessed before and after the intervention. Although there is a place for this kind of experimental comparison strategy in the evaluation of the outcomes of mental health services, it is usually not thought to be feasible in most service delivery settings. We will return to this comparison approach later and present some examples of its use in outcome evaluation. Suffice it to say here that experimental design is best justified in service delivery settings when a new or different treatment or program intervention is compared, through random assignment, to the "usual" or prior kind of treatment or service.

The vast majority of evaluation comparison strategies that are most acceptable in the broadest array of applied mental health settings, and those that are recommended here, have been called Preexperimental or Quasi-experimental Designs (Campbell & Stanley, 1963). The more research-oriented reader is referred to Campbell and Stanley's (1963) discussion of the Recurrent institutional cycle, or patched-up design, and Cook and Campbell's (1979) discussion of Cohort designs in formal and informal institutions with cyclical turnover for examples of use of inelegant comparisons to draw relatively rigorous conclusions. It is worth keeping in mind, when challenged by those of a purist scientific bent, that we are *not* primarily concerned with proving cause and effect, or proving that it is *the* treatment that is responsible for the change or differences observed.

We are generally primarily concerned with describing for decision makers or the public what consumers are like at the beginning of treatment or service, what they are like after having received service, and/or how they compare with some other groups on the same measures. Given the hundreds of laboratory efficacy studies that have proven that psychosocial interventions cause client changes, if field outcome evaluation studies produce similar change findings than it is plausible to conclude that it is the treatment or service that has probably caused the

TABLE 1   Characteristics of Evaluation Comparison Strategies

Strategy	Purpose	Strengths	Weaknesses
1. Single-cohort Pre–Posttest	Describe change	Acceptable to most providers	Weak evidence that treatment caused change.
2. Nonequivalent comparison groups			
a. Normative groups	Compare pre- and/or post-treatment status to status of a nonconsumer group.	Provides a static but meaningful nonconsumer reference point to aid in evaluating change data	Groups are likely to differ in many ways except for a few demographic characteristics (e.g., age).
b. Different setting groups	Compare change in one group with change in another group.	Provides a comparison group external to study group to aide interpreting data	Groups may differ in ways that affect outcomes; organization and population characteristics that affect outcomes may differ.
c. Same service setting groups	Same as 2.a.	Consumer and organizational variables of the groups likely to be similar	Groups may differ in ways that affect outcomes.
3. Experimental or randomized control groups	Prove that innovative service caused consumer change.	Eliminates many other explanations of the observed change	Is often unacceptable to providers; requires administrative logistic action.

changes. These comparisons are also helpful in providing program managers with information about differences in outcomes among different types or groups of consumers (e.g., diagnostic groups, gender groups).

The three primary types of evaluation comparisons, the single-cohort pretest–posttest comparison, the nonequivalent comparison group strategy and three variations of it, and the experimental or randomized control group design, will be discussed in the order of their acceptability from most to least acceptable in service delivery settings. The salient features of these five comparison strategies are summarized in Table 1. Recall that the most feasible designs also tend to be less certain with respect to "proving" that the treatment or intervention caused clients' changes. This is the feasibility–certainty trade-off mentioned earlier.

THE SINGLE-COHORT
PRETEST–POSTTEST COMPARISON

In this approach, description of change involves only one group of people that is selected in a consistent, systematic, and specified manner. The evaluation question addressed by this comparison is, Have the consumers changed significantly after having received treatment? If the outcome evaluation is to be for only a limited period of time in an outpatient clinic or an acute care inpatient unit, the cohort can be defined as all clients admitted during a particular time period. All members of the cohort are assessed at or near the time of admission and, minimally, again at or near the time of discharge from the service. Even though consumers are recruited into the cohort for a relatively brief time, in some outpatient clinics, for example, it may take many months for those receiving longer-term counseling to be discharged from treatment; that is, unless length of stay is rigidly prescribed to be short-term by policy or by reimbursement decisions.

If the effectiveness of outpatient treatment is to be evaluated in a setting in which long-term psychotherapy is done, termination assessments on all members of the cohort may be a long time coming. It may be more appropriate to target second or final assessments at some period prior to discharge, such as 6 or 12 months after admission, and still conduct a defensible outcome evaluation study. This will also reduce the number of clients for whom discharge assessments are missed. Recall that Howard, Kopta, Krause, and Orlinsky (1986) found that 50% of outpatients are improved after eight sessions and that 75% are improved after 26 sessions. Speer (1994) found that during-treatment assessments are reasonable proxies for discharge assessment that are missed for whatever reason, and that use of such proxy assessments may underestimate improvement rates by only 2%. Thus, in outpatient programs, considerable client improvement will be detected after the first 6 months of treatment.

For smaller scale programs with lower admissions rates, such as partial hospitalization or intensive case management for persistently and severely mentally ill consumers, it may be necessary to include all new admissions for an extended period, say 6–12 months, in order to develop a larger enough cohort to justify confidence in the findings. For example, McClary, Lubin, Evens, Watt, and Lebedum (1989) assessed 64 young chronic schizophrenic patients before discharge from the hospital and 9 months after entering an intensive case management program in the community. Case management significantly reduced readmission and hospital stay rates, and increased the percentage of medical appointments kept and hours of contact with staff.

Among programs with low turnover or discharge rates, such as for persistently and severely mentally ill older adults, it may not be realistic to target discharge as the time for the second or final assessment. Here, it may be more feasible to arbitrarily schedule the second assessment for 6 or 12 months and then evaluate client adjustment and change over this, albeit truncated, time period. An example here is Galligan's (1990) evaluation of a specialized residential unit and day treatment program for 36 intellectually challenged adults who also had psychiatric disorders. The clients were assessed at admission and after 1 year in the program. Galligan found that although there were substantial significant improvements on measures of independence, the 60% rate of weekly behavior problems suggested that most were not yet ready for movement to a less restrictive setting.

If outcome evaluation is to be implemented in a low-volume and low-discharge rate program that is already at its capacity, the evaluation may of necessity become a descriptive study of client change while receiving services rather than an outcome evaluation in an ultimate or posttreatment sense. Useful information might be obtained by comparing the changes among clients who have been in the program for, say, less than 6 months with those in the program for more than 6 months. Decisions such as these regarding the time intervals for assessments and data collection will need to be made within the context of the informational needs of those requesting the information for decision making purposes.

There are several other examples of descriptive single-cohort pretest-posttest outcome evaluation studies. Hugen (1993) evaluated the effectiveness of a 1-day psychoeducational workshop for 22 relatives of schizophrenic patients living in the community by assessing them 2 weeks before the workshop and 3 weeks after the workshop. There were significant improvements in knowledge of schizophrenia, family conflict, and relapse rates, but no changes in family attitudes toward schizophrenia or in family culpability for the illness. Johnson, Cline, Marcum, and Intress (1992) evaluated a 4-day, close-to-the-battle-zone crisis treatment program for 22 combat veterans with combat fatigue. They demonstrated significant decreases in anxiety, depression, and hostility; 21 of the 22 soldiers returned to duty. Leda and Rosenheck (1992) evaluated a domicillary program with psychiatric, rehabilitation, and substance abuse treatment for homeless mentally ill veterans, 81% of whom also had substance abuse diagnoses, via assessments at admission and 3 months postdischarge. They found significant improvements on psychiatric symptoms, alcohol and drug problems, social contacts, income, and employment. In a multiple cohort study of nursing home residents referred for mobile mental health services, Speer, O'Sullivan, and Lester (1996) found that the referral problems of 55% were much improved in the judgments of the service providers.

It should be noted that a weakness of the single cohort comparison strategy is that often there is no reference point external to the cohort to aid in interpreting findings. For example, in the Speer et al. (1996) study, provider ratings were used to determine that positive change had occurred among the majority of the members of the nursing home cohorts. However, it was not possible to determine how the improved residents compared with nonreferred nursing home residents or other people of the same age. This weakness can be alleviated by repeating the study in the same or a different setting (by replication) or by selection of appropriate measures, but the latter then moves the design into the cateory of nonequivalent comparison groups, which will be discussed next.

Finally, a word of caution is in order. In single-cohort designs, it is tempting to omit the admission assessment and to ask, for example, therapists or family members to make retrospective global judgments about the degree of change or problem resolution at some point after the conclusion of treatment or service (e.g., Assay & Dimperio, 1991; Lantican & Mayorga, 1993; Sluckin, Foreman, & Herbert, 1991). This demands almost perfect recall on the part of judges, comparison of recent behavior with retrospectively recalled prior behavior, and provides opportunity for judges to project their own subjectivity into the evaluation process. When significant time has passed, or when the clients' circumstances are unclear, therapist and providers tend to overestimate service effectiveness relative to that reported by clients and family members (e.g., Nicholson, 1989; also, see Chapter 6).

Another reason that pretreatment assessments are important is to determine whether the evaluation cohort is or is not like other consumers seen in the same setting, or receiving the same service. This is particularly important when consumers drop out of the evaluation at relatively high rates. Admission assessments are very useful for determining the representativeness of the cohort and the representativeness of consumers who fully participate in the evaluation. The reader is advised to avoid the posttreatment-assessment-only approach if at all possible; when single cohorts are used, admission *and* termination or follow-up assessments should be included.

NONEQUIVALENT COMPARISON GROUP STRATEGIES

The strength of these comparisons is that data from people outside of the cohort of primary interest are available for comparison purposes and to aid in interpreting the results. What distinguishes quasi-experimental comparisons from experimental design is that individuals are *not* randomly assigned to the different groups. Often, the cohort and the other group are preexisting groups perhaps organized or assessed for different purposes. The evaluation question being addressed is, Are consumers similar to or different than another group in meaningful ways before and/or after treatment? There are at least three kinds of nonequivalent comparison groups: those representing the normative group for particular assessment instruments, those from a different service setting, and those from within the same service delivery setting. These three comparison conditions will be described in order from greatest acceptability, least logistical effort, and greatest uncertainty to greater logistical effort and greater certainty of interpretation.

Normative Groups as Nonequivalent Comparison Groups

A neglected variation of nonequivalent comparison group designs is the use of the general population, or a nonpatient group, upon which an assessment instrument was standardized and which provides the norms for interpreting an individual's score, as a comparison group (e.g., Kazdin, 1994; Kendall & Grove, 1988). This is an instrument-specific "design" and depends totally on whether or not normative statistics, such as averages or means and standard deviations (a measure of how people distribute themselves or "scatter" around the group average), have been determined for a general public, "normal," or nonconsumer group for that specific measure.

Interpretation of the evaluation cohort's data is facilitated by comparing the mean or average scores of the clinical or treatment cohort with the mean of the normative or nonconsumer group, to determine whether or not they are different prior to treatment and whether or not they are still different after treatment. The standard deviation, or the measure of "scatter" of scores around the average score, can be used to examine this comparison. For example, in social and psychological research, two standard deviations above or below the normal group mean is commonly accepted as a statistical criterion suggesting deviance or probable pathology (e.g., Kendall & Grove, 1988). The scores between two standard deviations above, for example, and two standard deviations below the nonconsumer group average is often considered the normal range. If the mean and the standard deviation are provided for a particular assessment instrument, it is a matter of simply multiplying the standard deviation by two and then adding this number to the nonpatient mean and subtracting it from the mean to provide the numbers defining the outer limits of the normal range; or, defining the points above and below which significant differentness or deviance are suggested.

The admission average of the clinical cohort can then be compared to these numbers representing two standard deviations away from the nonconsumer mean in order to determine whether it is closer to the normal mean or closer to the number suggesting deviance. Or, the scores of the cohort members can be compared to the two standard deviation criterion to determine what proportion were "deviant" prior to the intervention. Given the occasional aspersion that recipients of outpatient treatment are largely the "worried well," it can be politically helpful to demonstrate that prior to receiving services consumers are significantly troubled in a statistical as well as a clinical sense.

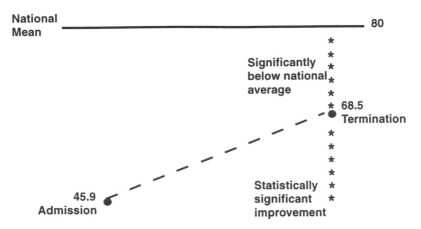

FIGURE 2   Well-being among older outpatients. N = 92; General Well-Being range, 0–110.

If the mean and standard deviation for a general public group are availabile, it is also a relatively simple arithmetic task to calculate t or z tests (available in any introductory statistics text) to determine whether or not the cohort and nonconsumer group means are reliably different. The availability of norms for an instrument permits several comparisons that can enhance communication of findings to nonscientist consumers of outcome evaluation results.

Another practical advantage of using a measure's norms as a comparison group is that it saves the time, energy, and cost of collecting assessments from another group for comparison purposes.

Two "shoestring" outcome evaluations conducted by the author provide examples of two different ways in which interpretation may be aided by norms. In a single-cohort, pretest–posttest study of change among 92 older adults in treatment at an outpatient mental health clinic, Dupuy's (1977) General Well-Being (GWB) scale was administered at admission and on several subsequent occasions including termination (Speer, 1994). Norms from a national probability sample of nearly 7000 adults are available for the GWB. The findings from this study are depicted in Figure 2. The cohort admission mean, which was exactly two standard deviations below the national sample mean, was also statistically reliably lower than the national sample mean indicating that this older outpatient cohort had significant well-being problems prior to treatment. The cohort's posttreatment mean was reliably greater than the pretreatment mean, indicating reliable improvement in well-being for the group. However, the posttreatment mean was also, still, statistically significantly below the national adult average. Thus, although there had been striking improvement while in treatment, the well-being of these older adults as a group was still appreciably poorer than the well-being of the average adult in the United States. Subsequent analyses indicated that 51% of the cohort had improved statistically, that 5% appeared to have worsened, and that consumers with major depression and adjustment disorders had significantly higher improvement rates than consumers with dysthymia.

In the study of supported housing for older adults with severe and persistent mental illness described earlier, one of the measures used was Cohen and Williamson's (1988) ten-item Perceived Stress Scale. Normative data from a national probability sample of over 1300 people are available, including data from nearly 300 persons 65 and older. The consumers were assessed on four occasions over a 2-year period. The results indicated that exactly half of the cohort reported stress greater than two standard deviations above the national older adult mean on one or more occasions. Although these older adults were very successful in staying out of inpatient care during the 2 years, they nonetheless experienced episodic severe stress (O'Sullivan & Speer, 1995). This degree of periodic distress has implication for quality of life, immune system health, and risk for depression.

These two outcome evaluation studies suggest an axiom for those contemplating evaluation of their mental health services with the assistance of instrument norms as a nonequivalent comparison group: such outcome evaluation studies often give the service the appearance of being less effective than it probably is. Such outcome evaluation findings often are somewhat awkward to explain to others; including the fact that some consumers probably become worse during treatment (Bergin first pointed out in 1966 that some consumers become worse while in treatment). Thus, there may be some political risk. However, as pointed out in Chapter 1, the alternative of not evaluating service results also has potentially severe adverse consequences. Helpful in this respect are Lipsey and Wilson's (1993) conclusions that psychological and behavioral interventions are as effective, or more effective in many instances, as medical interventions for physical illnesses. Candor regarding the limitations of service effectiveness may well contribute to subsequent credibility.

Although this subject overlaps with discussion in Chapter 4 on the selection of measuring instruments, it must be pointed out that it is very important that the instrument is significantly pertinent to the decision-making purposes that are driving the particular outcome evaluation. A measure should not be chosen just because it has norms; it must also be relevant to the purposes of the evaluation study. However, if two measures are available that seem to assess the same or similar characteristics, and one has norms and the other does not, the instrument with norms is clearly preferable.

Different-Setting Comparison Groups

Here the comparison group is selected from a different setting, usually for feasibility or cost reasons, but hopefully because the comparison group has something significant in common with the study group. This is usually a weaker comparison condition than same-setting comparison groups (see next section) because of the numerous system and organizational variables that may differ. Again, however, some reference point external to the study cohort is better than no reference point in interpreting the data.

A noteworthy example is the 5-year follow-up evaluation of an enhanced and subsequently defunded case management program for chronically mentally ill adults in one area in Colorado conducted by Shern et al. (1994). The comparison group was consumers from a similar case management program in a nearby geographic area of Colorado for which enhancements and defunding were not planned and did not occur. Findings indicated that program enhancements did increase the continuity of care and reduced unmet needs, and that the defunding of the enhancements 4 years into the program reversed these service delivery gains, relative to the comparison group. Another example is the previously mentioned evaluation of a demonstration supported housing program for older severely and persistently mentally ill adults by O'Sullivan and Speer (1995). The comparison groups were cohorts of Parkinson's disease patients and caregivers from whom repeated assessments over a 12-month period had been obtained using some of the same measures used to evaluate quality of life among the supported housing clients. The rationale for this decision was that the groups were about the same age, the Parkinson's patients also had a chronic illness, and the caregivers were dealing with a stressful situation (their spouse's Parkinson's disease). In spite of the differences of time, place, and setting, the Parkinson's groups provided some meaningful contrasts for the supported housing consumers.

Same Service Setting Comparison Groups

The ideal situation is when both groups are constituted within the same service delivery setting, and from the same consumer population. If planning time permits, data can be obtained from a cohort of clients prior to the implementation of a new or different program, and this group that received the prior service can be used as the comparison group for a new cohort that is exposed to the newly implemented service. An example is the evaluation of a new intensive community service program for state hospital dischargees reported by Bigelow, McFarland, Gareau, and Young (1991). Seventeen clients discharged from the hospital during the 2 months prior to beginning the new community program were specified as the comparison cohort and were assessed 2–3 months after discharge, as were the 25 clients discharged after the beginning of the new program. Although there was a mixture of positive differences and lack of differences between the two groups, the new program clients had a significantly lower rate of hospital re-use and distress scores, and significantly higher well-being and interpersonal relationship scores than the prior program consumers.

Although obtaining pre- and postservice assessment data on both groups provides the opportunity for a richer and more informed outcome evaluation, the two groups may permit meaningful evaluation on the basis of posttreatment-only assessment. An example is Hiday and Scheid-Cook's (1989) 6-month follow-up study of chronically mentally ill clients who were (a) committed to outpatient treatment, (b) involuntarily hospitalized, or (c) released from commitment. Although the group committed to outpatient care was significantly more involved in outpatient treatment than the other two groups, the three groups did not differ significantly on other outcome variables, such as number rehospitalized, days in hospital, arrests, social activities, and displays of dangerous behavior.

The riskiness, however, of follow-up-only or posttreatment-only assessment is exemplified by an outcome evaluation of persistently and severely mentally ill young adults who were involuntarily assigned to supported housing services and those who voluntarily requested such services (Brown, Ridgway, Anthony, & Rogers, 1991). The clients were followed up 9 months after entering the program. The involuntary consumers had significantly less time in independent living and lower ratings of residential stability. They also had higher rates of rehospitalization and postdischarge hospital days as a percentage of predischarge hospital days for 6-month periods. However, investigation of prestudy risk factors indicated that the involuntary group had significantly greater criminal records, rates of self-neglect, having been abused as children, domestic violence, family substance abuse, suicide attempts, homelessness, and medication noncompliance than the voluntary service-seeking client. Thus, the involuntary group was a substantially more troubled and at-risk group than those who voluntarily requested services. Although these data suggest that voluntary clients appear more successful, the total picture indicated that a substantial majority of the more at-risk involuntary consumers could nonetheless be successfully assisted by the program.

The Brown et al. (1991) outcome study also demonstrates the importance of obtaining as much information about the non-equivalent group clients as possible. More often than not the groups will differ on significant variables, and these differences will often determine how the results are interpreted and the conclusions drawn. This study also provides an example of creatively constituting the comparison group, here the voluntary group. These clients were retrospectively selected from a larger pool of clients who voluntarily sought services and were then followed up specifically as a comparison group for the involuntary clients. Outcome evaluation of community-based mental health services is often facilitated by imagination and creativity on the part of administrators and evaluators.

Another situation that lends itself to creation of a same setting comparison group is when the intervention under investigation can accommodate fewer consumers than the total number of people needing and requesting the service. An example is the evaluation of a structured 6-week substance abuse program in a jail by Peters, Kearns, Murrin, Dolente and May (1993). Many more inmates requested the program than could be accommodated by the available staff and space. Because those who could not be admitted had requested the service they were similar to the treated group on motivation to participate. These inmates who requested service but who could not be accepted into the program provided an excellent nonrandom comparison group.

An evaluation of an experimental desensitization-based treatment program for combat veterans with posttraumatic stress disorder by Solomon et al. (1992) provides an example of the importance of outcome evaluation. Forty consecutive veterans who were admitted into the program were compared with a like number selected from among those who received usual military treatment prior to the program. Follow-up of the two groups 9 months after treatment indicated that the groups did not differ on a number of variables, but the experimental group displayed *more* stress and psychological symptoms than did the comparison group. Thus, the new intervention appeared less effective than the usual treatment.

THE EXPERIMENTAL OR RANDOMIZED COMPARISON GROUP DESIGN

As indicated earlier, the design in which the study group is specified and the members then randomly assigned to the treatment or service of interest, or to some specified alternative, is the epitome of the scientific approach. The randomization process usually balances the two groups on variables that are not of interest to the evaluators but which nonetheless may affect the members of one group on the outcome variables. This is the risk taken when nonrandomized or naturally occurring (nonequivalent comparison groups) groups are used. The randomized comparison group design provides the strongest and most convincing evidence that it is the intervention of interest that has, in fact, caused the changes that we observe on the outcome measures. The evaluation question here is, Do consumers receiving the new service improve more than those receiving the alternative service after controlling for confounding influences (through randomization)? There are often a number of practical and apparent ethical issues that make it difficult for providers to accept and implement random assignment in their settings. The randomized experimental design, however, has been used appropriately and productively in a number of outcome evaluation studies.

For example, Clarkin, Glick, Haas, and Spencer (1991) studied the effectiveness of a new program of six psychoeducational sessions for family members of consumers currently receiving treatment in a psychiatric inpatient unit. The comparison condition was inpatient treatment as usual for the consumer (previously, family members had received no particular services). Family members who agreed to participate in the study were then randomly assigned to the psychoeducational program or to treatment as usual. At follow-up 6 months after the consumer was discharged, consumer functioning and symptoms and family attitudes toward treatment among the psychoeducational families were significantly better than among those who had received treatment as usual.

Henggler, Melton, and Smith (1992) conducted an experimental evaluation of an intensive in vivo family treatment and support services program for juvenile offenders. The comparison condition was the usual youth services provided for youthful offenders. Qualifying families were randomly assigned to either family treatment or usual services. Youth in the experimental program, as a group, had fewer arrests and days of incarceration, and higher family cohesion scores than did the usual services youth. Morse, Calsyn, Allen, Tempelhoff, and Smith (1992) reported an experimental evaluation of an assertive outreach and intensive case management program for homeless mentally ill persons, in which over 100 consumers were randomly assigned to intensive case management, a daytime drop-in center, or routine outpatient services at a mental health center. The case management consumers had significantly fewer homeless days than consumers in the other two services, but did not differ from other consumers on income, symptoms, self-esteem, or alienation.

As implied by these examples, usual or routine services can provide a meaningful and ethically acceptable alternative to a new or alternative service or treatment. In fact, "usual services" are becoming so common as a comparison condition that they now have their own acronym: TAU, which represents treatment as usual (e.g., Addis, 1997). The *no-treatment* control or comparison group alternative is for the most part now an irrelevant consideration. In the domain of psychotherapy research, psychosocial interventions have proven to be superior in effectiveness to no-treatment control conditions so frequently that there appears to be no need for further demonstration of this finding. There may still be a few situations where no-treatment comparison groups are meaningful, but probably not in mainstream service delivery settings. Arguments against random assignment in which depriving troubled people of treatment is used as the ethical basis for not randomizing is now generally a red herring. The field is now at the place where the pertinent and important question is, Is intervention X more effective than our usual way of serving or treating people with this problem and these characteristics? It is recommended that when consideration is being given to implementing a new or somewhat different treatment program that serious consideration be given to a randomized evaluation in which recipients of routine services are used as a comparison group.

REPORTING CONSUMER CHANGE

Although consumer change is the bottom line in outcome evaluation, specific methods for classifying consumers as significantly better or unchanged, or worse, are still controversial. Furthermore, the methodological approach I recommend involves somewhat more statistical manipulation and perhaps a greater need for consultive assistance than computations discussed thus far.

Nonetheless, there are at least three reasons why determining and reporting individual consumer change is important. The first general reason is that evaluators have the responsibility for reporting findings in ways that make sense and are comprehensible to nonscientist policy and decision makers. As mentioned earlier, one of the paradoxes of the mental health field is that there are volumes of research on the effectiveness of psychosocial interventions, psychotherapy, and counseling, which appear to have been of little interest or use to decision makers. A possible contributing factor is that researchers have not reported findings in ways that are "friendly" to nonscientists (Speer, 1994). For example, Smith, Glass and Miller (1980) summarized the effectiveness of psychotherapy literature by concluding that the average person who receives psychotherapy is better off at the end of treatment than 80% of people with similar problems who do not receive therapy. This also suggests that 20% of those who do not receive therapy are better off than the average therapy client, and that 20% of therapy clients are worse off at the end of treatment than the average untreated person. As recently as 1992, the effectiveness of psychotherapy was still being discussed in such terms (e.g., Weisz, Weiss, & Donenberg, 1992). I usually have to read such summary statements two or three times to be sure I understand what they are saying.

The second reason that determining individual consumer change is important was suggested by Jacobson and Truax (1991). They proposed that researchers have historically had difficulty interpreting *group* data to laypeople. The effectiveness implications of group averages, differences between group averages, and indices of how people distribute themselves around the averages have been hazy for nonstatisticians. That the averages of two groups differ, or that the average discharge score of a group differs from its average admission score does not seem quite specific enough.

The third reason for considering individual consumer change status can be thought of as a consumer care issue. Identification of people who appear to get worse will provide an impetus for potential program or treatment improvement.

AN EXAMPLE OF IMPROVEMENT
AND DETERIORATION RATES

The admission and discharge GWB data from a single cohort of over 90 older adult mental health outpatients that I previously reported (presented graphically above) exemplify one difficulty with group data (Speer, 1994). The average admission GWB score was significantly below the public average, and the average discharge score was significantly better than the admission average. So far, so good. However, the average discharge score was still significantly below the public average. How do we make sense of these findings? Fortunately, I did not have to try to explain these findings to state legislators or county commissioners.

The analysis of these data was carried one step further. Using a statistical method for testing the significance of the difference between the admission and the discharge scores of *individual* consumers, I determined the number who had reliably improved, those who had not changed significantly, and those whose discharge scores were reliably worse than their admission scores. Dividing these totals by the total number of consumers in the cohort indicated that 51% had improved, 44% were unchanged, and 5% appeared worse. Examination of the change rates by diagnosis indicated that 73% of consumers with major depression improved, 71% of those with adjustment disorders improved, but that only 53% of those with dysthymia improved. Furthermore, none of the consumers with major depression or adjustment disorders were classified as worse, whereas 9% of those with dysthymia appeared to have deteriorated.

These change rate data provide examples of how determining the significance of change of individual consumers can be used to "flesh out" the findings of tests of group differences and, it is hoped, convey more specific meaning to decision makers. The exact theoretical appropriateness of specific methods for testing the significance of individual consumer change is still being debated by academic methodologists (e.g., Hsu, 1995). However, a small group of studies using these methods suggest that among outpatients improvement rates in the 50–60% range and deterioration rates in the 5–10% range are common (e.g., Jacobson et al., 1984; Jacobson, Wilson, & Tupper, 1988). Findings reported by Speer and Greenbaum (1995) suggest that many of the methods for computing significant individual change scores produce change rates that are quite similar to one another from a practical standpoint.

THE RECOMMENDED METHOD

Although I have used a somewhat different method to evaluate the outcomes of outpatient services, the method recommended here is the Reliable Change Index (RCI) developed by Neil Jacobson and his colleagues (Jacobson & Truax,

1991). This method is not beyond scientific criticism. In keeping with the principle that relevance and utility to decision makers is preferred over scientific rigor and purity, the RCI is proposed as a standardized method. It will convey meaning about consumer change and facilitate comparisons across service settings. It is recommended here because there appear to be fewer theoretical methodological questions about it. This method is computationally more straightforward than other methods, and there is a small but growing literature on its use in reporting outcome change rates (Speer & Greenbaum, 1995). Although the formulas involved may appear intimidating to the nonstatistician, basic algebra will get the reader through them. The statistics needed for the computations are only the standard deviation of all consumers' admission scores, and a reliability coefficient that may be computed from the data or, in the instance of a standardized measure, can be found in the instrument's instruction manual. Internal consistency reliability (Cronbach's alpha) is recommended rather than test–retest reliability. These statistics, along with the consumer's admission and second occasion scores, will permit determination of whether the consumer's second occasion score was statistically better than his or her admission score, not different, or statistically poorer than the admission score. Two preliminary statistical steps are required. However, these two statistics only need to be computed once, and can be reused to test the significance of the changes for all consumers in the cohort.

The first step is computation of what is called the standard error (SE) of all consumers' admission scores. The formula is

$$SE = s_A (1 - r)^{1/2}, \tag{1}$$

where r is the reliability coefficient, and s_A is the standard deviation of all consumers' admission scores. To compute the SE, one subtracts the reliability coefficient from one, determines the square root of this number, and multiplies this square root number by the standard deviation of the admission scores. This is the SE.

The next step is computation of what is called the standard error of differences (SED). This formula is

$$SED = (2[SE]^2)^{1/2}. \tag{2}$$

This means that the SE from step one is squared, multiplied by two, and the square root is determined for the resulting number. This is the SED. Computation of SE is necessary to determine SED, which is used to test the significance of the change of individual consumers.

The significance of individual consumer's change is determined by computing the RCI by this formula:

$$RCI = (x_L - x_A)/SED, \tag{3}$$

where x_L is the consumer's last score, x_A is the consumer's admission score, and SED is the standard error of differences from equation 2. RCI is computed by simply subtracting the admission score from the consumer's last score and dividing by SED. If RCI is >1.96 the consumer is reliably better, if RCI is <–1.96 the consumer is reliably worse, and if RCI is between 1.96 and –1.96 the consumer has not changed significantly.

This is how the significance of the change of an individual consumer is determined. When one sets out to determine the change status of all consumers in a cohort, one proceeds a little differently. For each consumer's admission score, one calculates the score on the measure equivalent to RCI equal to 1.96 and equal to –1.96. Then, if the consumer's last score and the last score of all other consumers with the same admission score is or are greater than the score equivalent to 1.96, or less than the score equivalent to –1.96, those consumers have changed significantly. If their last scores are in between the score equivalent to 1.96 and –1.96, they have not changed significantly.

There are two ways to go about this process. If the organization has access to someone fluent in computer statistics, this person can use the computer to generate a whole table of upper and lower limit measure scores for each possible admission score. Then, a clerical or data entry person can simply enter the table, locate each consumer's admission score, and compare the consumer's last score with the upper and lower limit scores, and thus determine whether or not each consumer has changed significantly or not. If the organization does not have access to a computer person, the process can be done by hand with little trouble. An arithmetically inclined clerical person can be taught the simple arithmetic involved in calculating the measure scores equivalent to 1.96 and –1.96. Once this process is learned the change status of all the consumers in a 100-person cohort can be determined in a couple of hours. These calculations can then be retained for use with another cohort, assuming the same measure is used. Such tables of upper and lower limits for various measuring instruments could then be shared among different service agencies in the interest of saving time.

It should be noted that, technically, the criterion for significant change being used here is the amount of change greater than would be found by accident. That is, the change is greater than that which results from measurement error and accumulated random errors. However, it is unlikely that significant change determined in this manner will occur without some real consumer change (Jacobson & Truax, 1991).

DYSFUNCTIONAL VERSUS
NORMAL RANGES OF SCORES

Thus far, we have explored whether or not consumers have changed significantly. We have not determined where the consumer started or where he or she ended up with respect to people not seeking services (relative deviance). It will be useful to decision makers to know what proportion of consumers began in the dysfunctional range at admission and what proportion scored in the normal range on the measure at some later point in time. I am here talking about a cut-off point between the dysfunctional and normal ranges on a particular measure. Jacobson and Truax (1991), in the context of psychotherapy research, discuss several alternatives depending on whether or not nonconsumer norms are available for the measure, and depending on the extent of overlap of the distributions of admission and last scores. Because of my belief that measures with public norms should be used whenever possible, Jacobson's suggestion for instruments with norms will be discussed here. Jacobson suggests that a point two standard deviations from the general public mean (or average) be used as the cutoff point separating dysfunctionality and normality. Such a cutoff point is arguable, but is proposed as a standardized convention for outcome evaluation purposes. The two-standard-deviation point definition of "normality" and "abnormality" is not new; it has been used often in psychosocial research, most notably in relation to the original Minnesota Multiphasic Personality Inventory (MMPI). In outcome evaluation, O'Sullivan and Speer (1995) used this reference point to judge stress experienced by older adult consumers of supported housing services.

Jacobson and Truax (1991) have presented data demonstrating the use of significant change and the cutoff score definition of dysfunctionality among 30 couples who received marital therapy. One of the outcome measures used was the Dyadic Adjustment Scale. Prior to treatment, all 30 couples scored in the dysfunctional range. After treatment, 37% had neither improved significantly nor moved into the normal range; 30% had improved significantly, but their final score was still in the abnormal range; 33% had both improved significantly and moved into the normal range. One couple appeared to have deteriorated. Thus, although over 60% improved significantly, only half of this group (33% of the total cohort) improved significantly *and* scored in the normal range of functioning following treatment. This demonstrates the point that requiring positive change *and* "normality" can give the service program the appearance of quite modest effectiveness.

CAVEATS

This type of standardized measurement of change may be considered "soft" science and subject to criticism by scientific methodologists. However, determining what happened to how many people is a common approach in medicine and other applied sciences. What makes the scientific "purists" difficult to take seriously is that their criticisms are often at the theoretical level and are rarely supported by data. The little available comparative data suggest that some different approaches yield change rates that are not significantly different from one another (Speer & Greenbaum, 1995).

This suggested approach to measuring and reporting consumer change has several practical features that recommend it to practical outcome evaluation. First, it involves a standardized set of objective rules that alleviate some possible concerns about conflict of interest. Second, it produces results that can easily be translated into "improvement–deterioration" rates, which in turn should have meaning and potential utility for decision makers and practitioners alike. Third, the exemplifying change rates presented have a certain clinical credibility to them. Clinicians and practitioners know that not all their clients get better, that some improve significantly but still have problems, that, yes, a few do get worse or deteriorate while in treatment, and that some get better and then relapse. Differences in change rates by diagnosis also lend clinical credibility to the method and will also likely enhance the political credibility of outcome findings. Change rate findings may prove to be an important communication bootstrap that will permit more fruitful dialogue among policy makers, funders, evaluators, and service providers.

Returning to the matter of determining change rates when general public norms are *not* available, Jacobson suggests using a point two standard deviations from the admission mean (in the healthy or functional direction) as the cutoff point for normality. Little data exist using this approach. The potential difficulty is that change rates using this approach probably will not be comparable to those calculated on the basis of general public norms. However, we do need to learn more about this approach. Thus when evaluators use measures without nonconsumer norms, it is recommended that change data using this method be reported.

A complication in the calculation of improvement rates is that the rates are in part a function of the reliability of the measuring instruments used. Speer (1992) has reported findings indicating that even moderate decreases in reliability can dramatically lower improvement rates. It is strongly recommended that if calculations of change rates are contemplated, only measures with reliabilities of .75 or higher be used.

In order to avoid some unnecessary controversy, the distinction needs to be made between "significant change" as used here and "clinically significant change." Historically, Jacobson has called his evolving methodology for determining consumer change a method for determining "clinically significant change." I am concerned that this terminology may imply that methods such as those proposed here have been validated with other forms of clinical data; to my knowledge, they have not. Whether or not the RCI and moving into the "normal" range constitute *clinically* substantive change is a matter for futher research using methods appropriate for construct validation. What is proposed here is a method for determining change not likely to occur by accident, and which can be used as a perhaps temporary convention for helping to communicate and interpret outcome data to nonscientifically trained policy and decision makers.

ALTERNATIVES

The significant change method discussed here is most appropriate for use with questionnaires and psychosocial measuring instruments for which validity and reliability have been established. Such approaches, although relatively inexpensive, may not be appropriate for all decision makers or outcome evaluation situations. The selection of measures and methods should be driven by the decision maker's needs and the larger sociopolitical context. For example, self-report questionnaires may not provide data that is of most interest to funders and directors of substance abuse treatment programs. Here, variables such as abstinence as measured by urine tests may have greater credibility and importance. Posttreatment instances of family physical abuse may be of greater salience and worth than the families' responses on the Family Conflict scale of the Family Environment Scales.

Another alternative kind of significant change is the presence or absence of a psychiatric disorder. The NIMH Treatment of Depression Collaborative Research Program mentioned earlier provides an example of use of this type of outcome variable (Elkin, 1994). During the posttreatment follow-up phase of the study, the presence of major depression characteristics were used to classify consumers as relapsed or as continuing in remission. Because this type of assessment is usually based on a clinical interview, it is more expensive than other kinds outcome assessments. It may also be a stringent test of improvement.

"REGRESSION TO THE MEAN"

Sooner rather than later, the topic of regression to the mean will be raised in relation to single-cohort pretest-posttest and some nonequivalent comparison strategies, and in relation to determining the statistical reliability of individual consumer change. This is the purported phenomenon in which second (or later) assessments tend to be closer to the public average or more "normal" than the initial assessment. Regression to the mean has worried, particularly, clinical researchers (including this writer) for decades because it was believed that this statistical artifact would confound and obscure the study of human change. That is, the concern was that when consumers were assessed on two or more occasions some would appear to have improved because of regression to the mean rather than because they had really changed. Controversy about how to disentangle real human change from regression to the mean has been going on for nearly half a century and has often been heated. A number of methods have been proposed over the years to adjust for the "regression effect" but none have achieved wide acceptance.

During the 1980s, professor David Rogosa and his colleagues were doing important statistical and methodological work on the development of multiwave data analyses and growth curve methodology. In the process, the Rogosa group had to work through a number of traditional statistical principles that they came to consider myths, one of which was that regression to the mean is unique, universal, and important (Rogosa, 1988). Explication of the full rationale for this view is beyond the scope of this book (and the statistical capability of this author). Suffice it to say that regression to the mean is thought to be simply a manifestation of the well-known correlation between initial status and the magnitude of change, and is thus a tautology. The regression effect appears to be confounded by standardization induced by certain statistical definitions. More importantly, whether subsequent measures fall closer to or farther from the mean is determined by where the initial assessment falls on the overall change curve (Rogosa, Brandt, & Zimowski, 1982; Rogosa & Willett, 1985).

The writer is persuaded by the work of Rogosa and of Willett (1994) that when working with two assessment points (e.g., admission, discharge) difference scores are more reliable, meaningful and useful than traditionally believed; and that attempts to statistically adjust for purported regression to the mean create more logical and statistical problems than the straightforward analysis of simple pre- and postdifferences. Thus, the burden of proof should be on those who suggest that regression to the mean is a more plausible explanation of improvement following treatment than real consumer change.

In summary, a number of strategies have been described for collecting outcome information from consumer cohorts to facilitate the comparisons needed to evaluate consumer change. Related to these strategies, sources of comparative data have been described to assist in interpreting the outcome data and conveying its meaning to policy and program decision makers. These strategies have been presented in order from the simplest, involving the least administrative action, and having the greatest uncertainty in interpretation to the more complex, requiring greater management action and having greater certainty in interpretation. The potential value of a statistical method of determining reliable change of individual consumers for communication with decision makers has been discussed. A method based on the work of Jacobson was recommended and described. Limitations of and alternatives to this method were discussed. Potential criticisms based on the concept of regression to the mean were also discussed.

REFERENCES

Addis, M. E. (1997). Evaluating the treatment manual as a means of disseminating empirically validated psychotherapies. *Clinical Psychology: Science and Practice, 4,* 1–11.

Asay, T. P., & Dimperio, T. L. (1991). Outcome of children treated in psychiatric hospitals. In S. M. Mirin, J. T. Gossett, & M. C. Grob (Eds.), *Psychiatric treatment: Advances in outcome research* (pp. 21–30). Washington, DC: American Psychiatric Press.

Bergin, A. E. (1966). Some implications of psychotherapy research for therapeutic practice. *Journal of Abnormal Psychology, 71,* 235–246.

Bigelow, D. A., McFarland, B. H., Gareau, M. J., & Young, D. J. (1991). Implementation and effectiveness of a bed reduction project. *Community Mental Health Journal, 27,* 125–133.

Brown, M. A., Ridgway, P., Anthony, W. A., & Rogers, E. S. (1991). Comparison of outcomes for clients seeking and assigned to supported housing. *Hospital and Community Psychiatry, 42,* 1150–1153.

Campbell, D. T., & Stanley, J. C. (1963). *Experimental and Quasi-experimental Designs for Research.* Chicago: Rand McNally.

Clarke, R. T., Schaefer, M., Burchard, J. D., & Welkowitz, J. W. (1992). Wrapping community-based mental health services around children with a severe behavioral disorder: An evaluation of Project Wraparound. *Journal of Child and Family Studies, 1,* 242–261.

Clarkin, J. F., Glick, I. D., Haas, G., & Spencer, J. H. (1991). The effects of inpatient family intervention on treatment outcome. In S. M. Mirin, J. T. Gossett, & M. C. Grob (Eds.), *Psychiatric treatment: Advances in outcome research* (pp. 47–58). Washington, DC: American Psychiatric Press.

Cohen, S., & Williamson, G. (1988). Perceived stress in a probability sample of the United States. In S. Spacapan & S. Oskamp (Eds.), *Symposium on applied social psychology* (pp. 31–68). Newbury Park, CA: Sage.

Cook, T. D., & Campbell, D. T. (1979). *Quasi-experimentation: Design and analysis issues for field settings.* Chicago: Rand McNally.

Dupuy, H. J. (1977). *A concurrent validational study of the NCHS General Well-being Schedule* (DHEW Publication No. HRA 78-1347). Hyattsville, MD: National Centeer for Health Statistics, U.S. Department of Health, Education, and Welfare.

Elkin, I. (1994). The NIMH treatment of depression collaborative research program: Where we began and where we are. In A. E. Bergin & S. L. Garfield (Eds.), *Handbook of psychotherapy and behavior change* (4th ed., pp. 114–139). New York: Wiley.

Galligan, B. (1990). Serving people who are dually diagnosed: A program evaluation. *Mental Retardation, 28,* 353–358.

Henggeler, S. W., Melton, G. B., & Smith, L. A. (1992). Family preservation using multisystemic therapy: An effective alternative to incarcerating serious juvenile offenders. *Journal of Consulting and Clinical Psychology, 60,* 953–961.

Hiday, V. A., & Scheid-Cook, T. L. (1989). A follow-up of chronic patients committed to outpatient treatment. *Hospital and Community Psychiatry, 40,* 52–59.

Howard, K. I., Kopta, S. M., Krause, M. S., & Orlinsky, D. E. (1986). The dose-effect relationship in psychotherapy. *American Psychologist, 41,* 159–164.

Hsu, L. M. (1995). Regression toward the mean associated with measurement error and the identification of improvement and deterioration in psychotherapy. *Journal of Consulting and Clinical Psychology, 63,* 141–144.

Hugen, B. (1993). The effectiveness of a psychoeducational support service to families of persons with a chronic mental illness. *Research on Social Work Practice, 3,* 137–154.

Jacobson, N. S., Follette, W. C., Revenstorf, D., Baucom, D. H., Hohlweg, K., & Margolin, D. (1984). Variability in outcome and clinical significance of behavioral marital therapy: A re-analysis of outcome data. *Journal of Consulting and Clincial Psychology, 53,* 497–504.

Jacobson, N. S., & Truax, P. (1991). Clinical significance: A statistical approach to defining meaningful change in psychotherapy research. *Journal of Consulting and Clinical Psychology, 59,* 12–19.

Jacobson, N. S., Wilson, L., & Tupper, C. (1988). The clinical significance of treatment gains resulting from exposure-based interventions for agoraphobia: A reanalysis of outcome data. *Behavior Therapy, 19,* 539–552.

Johnson, L. B., Cline, D. W., Marcum, J. M., & Intress, J. L. (1992). Effectiveness of a stress recovery unit during the Persian Gulf war. *Hospital and Community Psychiatry, 43,* 829–831.

Kazdin, A. E. (1994). Methodology, design, and evaluation in psychotherapy research. In A. E. Bergin & S. L. Garfield (Eds.), *Handbook of psychotherapy and behavior change* (4th ed., pp. 19–71). New York: Wiley.

Kendall, P. C., & Grove, W. M. (1988). Normative comparisons in therapy outcome. *Beavioral Assessment, 10,* 147–58.

Knapp, M., Cambridge, P., Thomason, C., Beecham, J., Allen C., & Darton, R. (1994). Residential care as an alternative to long-hospital: A cost-effectiveness evaluation of two pilot projects. *International Journal of Geriatric Psychiatry, 9,* 297–304.

Lantican, L. S. M., & Mayorga, J. (1993). Effectiveness of a women's mental health treatment program: A pilot study. *Issues in Mental Health Nursing, 14,* 31–49.

Leda, C., & Rosenheck, R. (1992). Mental health status and community adjustment after treatment in a residential treatment program for homeless veterans. *American Journal of Psychiatry, 149,* 1219–1224.

Lipsey, M. W. & Wilson, D. B. (1993). The efficacy of psychological, educational, and behavioral treatment: Confirmation from meta-analysis. *American Psychologist, 48,* 1181–1209.

McClary, S., Lubin, B., Evans, C., Watt, B., & Lebedun, M. (1989). Evaluation of a community treatment program for young adult schizophrenics. *Journal of Clinical Psychology, 45,* 806–808.

Morse, G. A., Calsyn, R. J., Allen, G., Tempelhoff, B., & Smith, R. (1992). Experimental comparison of the effects of three treatment programs for homeless mentally ill people. *Hospital and Community Psychiatry, 43,* 1005–1010.

Nicholson, S. (1989). Outcome evaluation of therapeutic effectiveness. *The Australian and New Zealand Journal of Family Therapy, 10,* 77–83.

O'Sullivan, M., & Speer, D. C. (1995). *The Supported Housing Program, Broward County Elderly Services, Ft. Lauderdale, FL: Evaluation Final Report.* Tampa, FL: Florida Mental Health Institute.

Peters, R. A., Kearns, W. D., Murrin, M. R., Dolente, A. S., & May, R. L. (1993). Examining the effectiveness of in-jail substance abuse treatment. *Journal of Offender Rehabilitation, 19,* 1–39.

Rogosa, D. (1988). Myths about longitudinal research. In K. W. Schaie & S. C. Rawlings (Eds.), *Methodological issues in aging research* (pp. 171–209). New York: Springer.

Rogosa, D., Brandt, D., & Zimowski, M. (1982). A growth curve approach to the measurement of change. *Psychological Bulletin, 92,* 726–748.

Rogosa, D. R., & Willett, J. B. (1985). Understanding correlates of change by modeling individual differences in growth. *Psychoimetrika, 50,* 203–228.

Shern, D. L., Wilson, N. Z., Coen, A. S., Patrick, D. C., Foster, M., Bartsch, D. A., & Demmler, J. (1994). Client outcomes II. Longitudinal client ourcome data from the Colorado treatment outcome study. *Milbank Quarterly, 72,* 123–148.

Sluckin, A., Foreman, N., & Herbert, M. (1991). Behavioural treatment programs and selectivity of speaking at follow-up in a sample of 25 selective mutes. *Australian Psychologist, 26,* 132–137.

Smith, M. L., Glass, G. V., & Miller, T. I. (1980). *The benefits of psychotherapy.* Baltimore: Johns Hopkins University Press.

Solomon, Z., Shalev, A., Spiro, S. E., Dolev, A., Bleich, A., Waysman, M., & Cooper, S. (1992). Negative psychometric outcomes: Self-report measures and a follow-up telephone survey. *Journal of Traumatic Stress, 5,* 225–246.

Speer, D. C. (1992). Clinically significant change: Jacobson and Truax (1991) revisited. *Journal of Consulting and Clinical Psychology, 60,* 402–408.

Speer, D. C. (1994). Can treatment research inform decision makers? Nonexperimental method issues and examples among older outpatients. *Journal of Consulting and Clinical Psychology, 62,* 560–568.

Speer, D. C., & Greenbaum, P. E. (1995). Five methods for computing significant individual client change and improvement rates: Support for an individual growth curve approach. *Journal of Consulting and Clinical Psychology, 63,* 1044–1048.

Speer, D. C., O'Sullivan, M. J., & Lester, W. A. (1996). Impact of mental health services in nursing homes: The clinicians perspective. *Journal of Clinical Geropsychology, 2,* 83–92.

Weisz, J. R., Weiss, B., & Donenberg, G. R. (1992). The lab versus the clinic: Effects of child and adolescent psychotherapy. *American Psychologist, 47,* 1578–1585.

Willett, J. B. (1994). Measuring change more effectively by modeling individual growth over time. In T. Husen & T. N. Postlethwaite (Eds.), *The international encyclopedia of education* (2nd ed., pp. 1–9). Oxford, UK: Pergamon Press.

CHAPTER 4

What Should Be Measured? Issues

One would think that the answer to this question should be relatively straight-forward. A reasonable line of thinking would be determine why treatment services were sought for an individual and then determine whether or not the individual is different on this concern after having received treatment. Unfortunately, reality is not as reasonable as we would wish. One of the consequences of the neglect of outcome evaluation until recently is a lack of well- developed, outcome evaluation-friendly, standardized measures, with general public norms for the variety of reasons that people seek mental health services. An area in which measure development has a strong historical tradition is psychology, where a lot of effort has gone into the development and standardization of self-report tests and questionnaires. Usually these instruments were developed for reasons other than the evaluation of mental health services. The field of psychology, however, has been an active participant in the psychotherapy research movement mentioned earlier. This has provided the impetus for the development of some measures that lend themselves to outcome evaluation efforts. In recent years, a number of outcome evaluation measures have evolved from national health survey work (e.g., the SF-36, Ware, Snow, Kosinski, & Gandek, 1993) and large-scale mental health services research (e.g., The COMPASS system, Sperry, Brill, Howard, & Grissom, 1996). Some of these measures will be discussed in Chapter 5.

As a result evaluators are confronted with a wide variety of measures, developed for a variety of reasons, and of varying quality from a standardization, psychometric and normative point of view. Evaluators are often confronted with difficult decisions in selecting measurement instruments for outcome evaluation work.

WHAT TO MEASURE

In considering *what* to measure one is immediately confronted with an array of options that various evaluators and researchers have considered important for various reasons in a variety of settings. From a psychiatric standpoint, a reasonable question is whether or not the symptoms characterizing a person's problems at admission are better or improved after treatment: Is Mr. Jones less depressed, is he still hallucinating, is he still assaulting his wife, and is he socializing with friends and family now? Related to symptoms is the person's psychiatric disorder or diagnosis. Following treatment, does the person still display the behavior typifying major depression?

Because most reasons for receiving mental health services included varying degrees and types of distress, pain, apprehension, or discomfort, measures of distress are often considered pertinent to whether or not treatment has been helpful or beneficial. Here measures often overlap symptom measures such as depression, anxiety, or panic. Other variants of distress include general well-being, self-esteem or self-confidence, stress, loneliness, quality of life, self-perceived health, and "subsyndromal" or "minor" depression (a phenomenon currently receiving renewed attention in geriatric mental health).

An outcome domain that is receiving increasing governmental attention, particularly with respect to public-sector mental health services, is consumer functioning or the person's ability to perform ordinary activities of daily living and common role behaviors. A prominent question is, Is the person employed and can he or she support him or herself financially? Related work role behavior includes going to work on a regular basis and performing satisfactorily from the employer's standpoint. For children, this type of role functioning translates into attending, adapting to, and learning in school.

Other role-functioning dimensions include homemaking and self-care tasks such as personal hygiene, ability to shop for groceries, doing laundry, use of public transportation, making and keeping medical appointments, and management of one's financial matters. Social activities and recreational activities outside of the home are often considered important aspects of personal functioning, as is the ability to get along with and interact with other people. In the substance abuse domain, abstinence is highly relevant, as are maintenance of employment, health, and family relationships.

Because social support appears central to many dimensions of human adjustment, such as protection against depression, as a means of managing stress and coping, and being conducive to health and longevity (e.g., Lin, Dean, & Ensel, 1986; Schwarzer & Leppin, 1989), the presence of and ability to maintain a supportive social network are often viewed as important outcome variables. Also from a social systems perspective, the effects of the person's problems on others may be important outcome considerations. Examples include whether or not the spouse and children are being battered, the stress and depression levels of family members, and the burden or stress experienced by those responsible for the care and support of person with the mental health problems.

Athough unanimity does not exist, *there is an emerging consensus that the basic elements of outcome assessment should include measures of distress, symptoms, and functioning.* Freedom from inordinate pain and the ability to care for oneself seem to be minimum considerations.

Another outcome measure perspective, and one with potentially important funding implications, is the purpose and mission for which the provider entity is being funded. Here we are talking about the goals and objectives for which funds are being provided. In an agency that provides case management services for persons with severe and persistent mental illness, for example, reduction of expensive rehospitalizations and hospital lengths of stay may be important outcome considerations. If a provider is under contract to a large employer to provide mental health services for employees, indicators like work performance, absence from work, and amount of sick leave used may be cogent outcome issues.

CLIENT SATISFACTION, OUTCOME MEASURE, OR INDEX OF QUALITY OF CARE?

In the context of service outcome evaluation, consumers' feedback about their satisfaction with how they were dealt with and the services they received needs to be addressed. Consumer advocacy groups have done the field a great service by demanding the respectful, humane, and efficient provision of services, and by demanding that provider organizations monitor how consumers feel about how they are treated.

From the standpoint of treatment or service outcomes, I view client satisfaction as an index of quality of care rather than as an outcome measure. The history of the relationship between measures of satisfaction and measures of outcome has been very inconsistent. For a number of years early in the development of program evaluation for mental health, a consistent finding was *no* relationship between satisfaction and outcome. That is, whether or not a client was pleased with the services he or she received seemed to have little to do with whether or not the consumer benefited from the service.

In recent years, findings of a positive relationship between satisfaction and outcome have begun to emerge. A better understanding of the relationships between these variables is needed. For current purposes, however, client satisfaction will not be considered as a treatment outcome or effectiveness measure (it may be considered an important index of the professionalism of the provider and the provider organization, or as index of quality of care, however).

THE QUALITY OF LIFE CONCEPT

A topic that is receiving considerable current attention is the global concept quality of life. This is a particular concern for consumers with severe and persistent mental illness and their families. A variety of instruments have been and are being developed to assess consumers' quality of life. However, quality of life usually involves multiple dimensions, and measures usually include a variety of subscales and questions. Quality of life can be thought of as including all or a combination of personal sense of well-being, distress, satisfaction with housing and/or income, one's perceived health, feeling safe, social networks, and satisfaction with social support, and so on. Because quality of life is an umbrella concept, it does not appear to have a single measure that operationalizes it. For purposes of this discussion, we will focus on the multiple subdimensions that are often used to assess consumers' quality of life.

SINGLE OR MULTIPLE MEASURES?

Early psychotherapy research was criticized because of heavy reliance on single-outcome measures. Increasing sophistication and improved technology have led to the now obvious view that a single measure cannot capture the multiple important aspects of human adjustment and functioning. Furthermore, almost all of the outcome evaluation and research studies cited below amply demonstrate the fact that consumers are inclined to improve in some respects, to not change in other areas, and occasionally become worse on other dimensions of adjustment and functioning. Use of a single or very limited number of measures creates the risk of missing important information about the consequences of service programs. A recently emerging example is provided by the outcome studies of case management services for severely and persistently mentally ill adults. One consistent finding is that these services are very effective in helping consumers avoid hospitalization, and in minimizing hospital stays. Another consistent finding is that these services are relatively impotent in reducing consumer distress and symptoms, and in enhancing community functioning (Speer & Newman, 1996). A limited array of measures might have missed this important discrepancy of findings. Another example is the Clarke, Schaefer, Burchard, and Welkowitz (1992) study of intensive family and school "wrap-around" treatment services for severely maladjusted children and youth. The results were that the youth improved significantly at home but not at school. Failure to assess adjustment in either setting would have led to highly misleading conclusions.

The answer to the question, What should we measure? is to assess adjustment and functioning in as many different service- relevant domains as is feasible.

IN WHOSE OPINION?

Given this wide array of human conditions and behaviors, and agency and provider missions, further complicating the decision- making process is whose perspective is most appropriate. In 1977, Professor Hans Strupp and Dr. Hadley published a paper entitled, "A tripartite model of mental health and therapeutic outcomes" (see also, Strupp, 1996). Strupp and Hadley proposed that there are at least three stakeholders, with different perspectives, who have inherent interests in the helpfulness and effectiveness of psychotherapy (I would add that these interests also pertain for most mental health services). They went on to postulate that the three different stakeholders also have different but intrinsically valid points of view on whether or not mental health services are effective. First, they suggest, is that the *client* is absolutely the best judge of his or her own pain, distress, or discomfort. Second, the *community* or society, including family members, neighbors, employers, law enforcement officals, and so on, are probably the best judges of the client's functioning or role performance behaviors, and conformity to social rules and norms. Third, they posited that the *therapist* is the best judge of changes in the client's psychopathology or internal psychological functioning. Strupp and Hadley stated that comprehensive assessment of the effectiveness of treatment should include all three perspectives.

In 1996, funders of public mental health services appear to have little interest in therapists' views, and, in some sectors, are skeptical of therapist- or clinician-provided outcome data. Third-party payers and managed care entities, on the other hand, seem satisfied with only therapist-provided diagnoses, treatment plans and goals, and views regarding consumer change or progress.

AN OUTCOME MEASURE FRAMEWORK

Given this variety of measurement issues, and opinions about appropriate sources of outcome information, how do we proceed? An expanded and modified

TABLE 2   A Measurement Variable by Data Source Framework

Source	Distress	Symptoms, disorder, diagnosis	Functioning, role performance
Client	A	B	c
Significant others	d	e	F
Public gatekeepers	g	h	I
Independent observers	j	K	l
Therapists/providers	m	N	o

Struppian matrix, as one organizing conceptual framework, is presented in Table 2. Currently, disorders and diagnoses appear to be of more interest to funding and policy decision makers than does Strupp's category of psychopathology. The client is the person seeking or for whom mental health services are sought. Significant others are those people upon whom the client's behavior or adjustment may impact, and includes, for example, family members, employer, neighbors, friends, and landlords. Public gatekeepers are often community persons with some form of offical or civil responsibilities, but who do not have a personal stake in or social relationship with the client. Such persons would include law-enforcement personnel, hospital emergency room or crisis stabilization unit staff, medical examiners, court officials, bank officials, protective services staff, and so on. These people are thought of as not having a vested personal interest in the client; their interests are of a professional or detached nature. Independent observers are professional or specially trained persons, not members of the service provider organization, competent to perform specific kinds of assessments and with no personal interest in either the client or the provider. Therapists and providers are the purveyors of the mental health services.

Theoretically, all of the source persons could be asked to provide information or views about all three types of information (distress, symptoms, disorders, and diagnoses, and functioning and role performance). I believe, however, that those row–column intersections with a capitalized letter printed in bold are the best sources of information about that particular aspect of the client's behavior or adjustment (A, B, F, I, K, and N). Even among these highlighted cells, some sources may be more appropriate than others. Issues considered here include possible biases, and time, place, situation, and circumstance opportunities to observe different aspects of the client's behavior in various settings.

OWNERSHIP OF MEASURES

A mundane issue that new evaluators need to be aware of is who owns the instrument. Most of the measures reported in the research and evaluation literature, and most described in Chapter 5, are in *the public domain*. That is they are not copyrighted, and the authors or creators are not claiming proprietary ownership of the instruments. This means that the measures may be used by anyone free of charge and without the author's permission. A few other measures, however, have copyrights, are *proprietary* instruments, and therefore are not free. Usually the rights to reproduce the instrument have been sold to publishers, and the manuals, questionnaires, and/or answer sheets must be purchased; sometimes, only the publisher can score the measures, for a fee.

If use of the instrument must be purchased, this may or may not be a major expense, depending on the available evaluation budget. For small-scale evaluations, this would be a minor expense. The costs involved for large-scale or ongoing evaluations might force the planners of the evaluations to carefully think through the specific need for the specific proprietary instrument. One of the most widely used symptom measures, The Hopkins Symptom Checklist-90, is such a copyrighted instrument, and its use must be purchased. At this writing, it appears that the Subjective Well-Being Scale and the Current Symptoms Scale of the Compass Treatment System (Sperry et al., 1996) are proprietary and their use must be purchased. However, a number of excellent instruments with norms are available in the public domain (e.g., Dupuy's [1977] General Well-Being Scale and Cohen and Williamson's [1988] Perceived Stress Scale).

Occasionally test publishers are willing to waive charges or grant permission to use a measure or portions thereof for reduced costs, under specific circumstances. These circumstances usually involve the user being a not-for-profit entity, the use being for evaluation research purposes, and the use being limited, such as the desire to use only one or two subscales from a larger multiscale instrument. Such waivers, if granted, are usually for relatively brief and specified periods of time and/or for very specific purposes. Such waivers must be obtained in writing by corresponding with the publisher.

In this chapter, issues pertaining to selection of measures have been discussed. These have included the topic of client satisfaction, multiple measures, and the perspectives of different stakeholders in the mental health service process.

REFERENCES

Clarke, R. T., Schaefer, M., Haas, G., & Welkowitz, J. W. (1991). Wrapping community-based mental health services around children with a severe behavioral disorder: An evaluation of Project Wraparound. *Journal of Child and Family Studies, 1,* 242–261.

Cohen, S., & Williamson, G. (1988). Perceived stress in a probability sample of the United States. In S. Spacapan & S. Oskamp (Eds.), *The social psychology of health: Claremont symposium on applied psychology* (pp. 31–68). Newbury Park, CA: Sage.

Dupuy, H. J. (1977). *A concurrent validational study of the NCHS general well-being schedule* (DHEW Publication No. HRA 78-1347). Hyattsville, MD: National Center for Health Statistics, U.S. Department of Health, Education and Welfare.

Lin, N., Dean, A., & Ensel, W. (1986). *Social support, life events, and depression.* New York: Academic Press.

Schwarzer, R., & Leppin, A. (1989). Social support and health: A meta-analysis. *Psychology and Health, 3,* 1–16.

Speer, D. C., & Newman, F. L. (1996). Mental health services outcome evaluation. *Clinical Psychology: Science and Practice, 3,* 105–129.

Sperry, L., Brill, P. L., Howard, K. I., & Grissom, G. R. (1996). *Treatment outcomes in psychotherapy and psychiatric interventions.* New York: Brunner/Mazel.

Strupp, H. H. (1996). The tripartite model and the *Consumer Reports* study. *American Psychologist, 51,* 1017–1024.

Strupp, H. H., & Hadley, S. M. (1977). A tripartite model of mental health and therapeutic outcomes. *American Psychologist, 32,* 187–96.

Ware, J. E., Snow, K. K., Kosinski, M., & Gandek, B. (1993). *SF-36 Health Survey: Manual and Interpretation Guide.* Boston: The Health Institute, New England Medical Center.

CHAPTER 5

What Should Be Measured? Instruments

This chapter will not be a comprehensive review of all available measures; instead, instruments with which I am familiar are presented as examples. Readers who are interested in a comprehensive listing of psychological measures are referred to The Mental Measurement Yearbook series (e.g., Conoley & Impara, 1995). Other important sources for mental health outcome assessments are *The 1996 Behavioral Outcomes & Guidelines Sourcebook* (1995) and *Outcomes Assessment in Clinical Practice* (Sederer & Dickey, 1996). The Struppian framework presented in Chapter 4, depicting consumer distress, symptoms, and disorders, and role functioning from the perspective of various observers, will be used to organize the discussion of potential outcome measures.

CLIENTS' SELF-REPORTS OF DISTRESS

We begin with Cell A in Table 2. For outcome evaluation purposes, I concur with Strupp that the inherently most appropriate reporter of the client's pain, discomfort, or distress is the client him or herself. There may be circumstances in which other sources of views about clients' distress may be considered (e.g., when the consumer is so withdrawn and verbally unresponsive that self-report is not possible). Discussion of kinds of distress that are also thought of as being symptoms of a psychiatric disorder will be deferred to the next section. Kinds of distress not usually thought of as symptomatic will be presented here.

An excellent but little used broad-spectrum instrument is Dupuy's (1977) *General Well-Being* (GWB) scale. This is an 18-item, self-administering questionnaire that takes adults less than 5 minutes to complete. It has the further advantage of having normative data available from a randomly selected national sample of nearly 7000 adults. The GWB has demonstrated reliability and validity. In spite of being a composite measure of depressive affect, anxiety, stress, physical well-being, and sense of emotional control, it has excellent internal reliability (its items correlate with one another very well). An example of its use is provided in Speer's (1994) study of older adult outpatients. Because of its extensive range, 0–110, there is plenty of room for clients to display improvement as well as deterioration. The GWB can be thought of as a broad index of satisfaction with self and/or quality of life.

Sperry, Brill, Howard, and Grissom (1996) have recently reported a four-item self-report *Subjective Well-Being* scale, with excellent internal reliability, test–retest reliability, and concurrent validity (the extent to which the scale correlates with other similar measures). Although norms based on a large group of outpatients at admission, and a statistically generated "expected course of recovery" are available, nonconsumer norms are apparently not available.

Another broad-spectrum measure of distress that is rising in popularity in mental health services research is the five-item Mental Health scale of the SF-36 instrument (Ware, Snow, Kosinski & Gandek, 1993; Ware & Sherbourne, 1992). This scale assesses heterogeneous well-being, distress, and symptoms. The SF-36 and its eight-component scales were developed during the 1980s for use in a national medical outcome study. Both the SF-36 and the Mental Health scale are self-administering, self-report measures for which age- and gender-stratified national public norms are available (Ware et al., 1993). The other seven basic scales are physical functioning, role limitations due to physical problems, social functioning, bodily pain, role limitations due to emotional problems, vitality, and general perceptions of personal health. More recently, additional work with the SF-36 has produced a physical component summary scale and a 14-item mental health component summary scale (Ware, Kosinski, & Keller, 1994). Because of its brevity and the extensive normative data available, this instrument should receive consideration in selecting outcome measures. The one potential weakness of the Mental Health scale is that it is heterogeneous in content, rather than assessing a specific dimension such as depression, anger, or social support. In this sense, it is like a measure of broad-spectrum well-being. Its norms, however, permit assessment of relative deviance.

Another nonsymptom measure of malaise is Cohen and Williamson's (1988) Perceived Stress Scale (PSS). A flexible feature of this instrument is that it is available in 4, 10, and 14-item forms, all of which have norms from a randomly selected national sample of over 2000 adults. A useful feature of the norms is that they are reported by gender, age group, income level, education, and ethnic group. Sample items are "In the last month, how often have you been upset because something unexpected happened?" and "In the last month, how often have you felt difficulties were piling up so high that you could not overcome them?" The response options are a five-point rating scale ranging from "never" to "very often." The scales have good reliability and have considerable demonstrated validity. The four-item scale lends itself to by-mail follow-up questionnaires, whereas the 10- and 14-item versions could be used for on-site assessments. An example of the use of the PSS is O'Sullivan and Speer's (1995) study of older adults with severe and persistent mental illness who were consumers of supported housing services.

Although *social support* (or the absence thereof) is not usually thought of as an index of distress, its reverse relationship with other measures of psychological distress and illness and its clinical face validity suggest it for consideration as an important client self-report outcome measure. Two well- developed and standarized measures of social support are the Interpersonal Support Evaluation List (ISEL; Cohen, Mermelstein, Kamarck, & Hoberman, 1985), and the Perceived Social Support from Friends and Family scales (PSSFF; Procidano & Heller, 1983). Both of these instruments have good reliability and validity, are self-administering, brief, and have subscales that assess different aspects of social support. Their primary limitation is that they do not have norms available. Nonetheless, they could be useful in pretreatment–posttreatment or repeated measures evaluations if interest is largely in demonstrating change in perceived support as a consequence of the intervention.

Another potentially useful nonsymptom outcome instrument is the Social Skills Inventory (Riggio, 1986), which assesses several dimensions of interpersonal behavior, such as emotional expressivity, emotional control, and social sensitivity. Again, the instrument is well developed, has excellent reliability and validity, and differentiates men and women in expectable ways. Its limitation, too, is the absence of norms.

CLIENTS' SELF-REPORTS OF SYMPTOMS

Several measures of client mental health or psychiatric symptoms are also indicators of distress. The most widely used self-administering self-report measures of symptoms for program evaluation purposes, and those recommended by the writer, are the Hopkins Symptom Checklist-90-Revised (SCL-90-R) (Smith, 1996) and its companion short form the Brief Symptom Inventory (BSI) (Smith, 1996). Both instruments consist of the same nine-symptom scale and three global or summary score scales. Both instruments have norms from over 900 nonpatients. There are 90 items on the SCL-90, with items per scale ranging from 6 to 13. The BSI has 53 items, with a range of 5–7 items per scale. The SCL-90 takes about 30 minutes to complete and the BSI about 15 minutes. The scales of both instruments have good internal and test–retest reliability, and both have extensively researched validity. A limitation is that both instruments are copyrighted, and the manuals and questionnaire answer sheets must be purchased. As a result, the cost will be somewhat greater than for other instruments.

The nine individual symptom scales, in both instruments, are

Somatization
Obsessive-compulsive
Interpersonal Sensitivity
Depression
Anxiety
Hostility
Phobic Anxiety
Paranoid Ideation
Psychoticism

The symptom dimensions assessed are largely those suggested by the scale names. The exception is the Interpersonal Sensitivity scale, which assesses feelings of personal inferiority, inadequacy, and discomfort during interpersonal interactions. Thus, it taps a sense of insecurity and low self-esteem.

The Depression, Anxiety, and Interpersonal Sensitivity scales are obviously the most direct symptom measures of distress and psychological pain. The Hostility scale has implications for the well-being of others in the client's environment. Examples of use of these instruments in outcome evaluation are provided in Henggeler, Melton, and Smith's (1992) experimental study of family therapy for juvenile offenders and their families, Lehman, Postrado, Roth, McNary, and Goldman's (1994) study of case management for adults with chronic mental illness, and Speer and Swindle's (1982) study of adult outpatients in a community mental health center.

Another recently developed and reported symptom checklist is the self-administering 40-item Current Symptoms scale (Sperry et al., 1996). Each item is rated on a five-point scale, on the basis of the frequency with which the symptom is experienced. This instrument consists of seven scales linked to the most frequently occurring Diagnostic and Statistical Manual of Mental Disorders IV (DSM-IV; APA, 1994) diagnoses among outpatients: adjustment disorder, anxiety, bipolar, depression, obsessive-compulsive, phobia, and substance use. The scales have good internal consistency (with a couple of exceptions) and good test–retest reliability. Nonconsumer norms are apparently not available, and the instrument has a narrower range of mental health problems than does the SCL-90, for example.

There are two self-administering depression scales that have been widely used in mental health research. The Center for Epidemiologic Studies-Depression Scale (CES-D; Radloff, 1977) is a 20-item scale with each item being rated on a four-point scale. The scale has adequate internal consistency, test–retest reliability, and validity. Its main weakness is the lack of norms. The other scale is the Geriatric Depression Scale (GDS), widely used among older adults (Yesavage & Brink, 1983). The GDS is a 30-item, yes–no scale that is simpler in its response format than the CES-D. An advantage is that it is also available in a 15-item short form that correlates very well with the longer form (Sheikh & Yesavage, 1986). The GDS has been extensively researched in recent years and appears to be a solid instrument. Although it too lacks large-scale norms, the mean and standard deviation from a validation group of 40 older adults with no history of mental health problems are available for comparison purposes (Yesavage & Brink, 1983). Three recent studies indicate that it can be administered to a consumer over the telephone, and by interview to nursing home residents, with validity and reliability results equal to those of self-administration (Burke, Roccaforte, Wengel, Conley, & Potter, 1995; Morishita et al., 1995; Parmelee & Katz, 1990). Both the CES-D and the GDS have recommended cutoff scores that suggest the possible presence of severe depression and indicate that further clinical evaluation is in order.

A word about the Minnesota Multiphasic Personality Inventory-2 is in order (MMPI-2; Graham, 1990). The MMPI is probably the most widely used clinical test available. Although self-administering, it is a very lengthy test requiring 1 to $1\frac{1}{2}$ hours to complete. Its scales do in fact appear to measure personality characteristics and psychopathology. Although of considerable diagnostic and treatment planning utility, its findings are awkward to interpret to policy and funding decision makers. Because several scales appear to assess personality traits, which may be less amenable to short-term change than measures of other consumer behaviors, caution and careful consideration are recommended in using the MMPI-2 for outcome evaluation purposes. The MMPI is another proprietary instrument for which the materials must be purchased.

CLIENTS' SELF-REPORTS OF FUNCTIONING AND ROLE PERFORMANCE

The appropriateness and validity of assessing consumer functioning by means of self-report is unclear. There is some evidence that persistently and severely mentally ill consumers may overestimate their levels of functioning on some dimensions relative to the perceptions of their family members and case managers. Massey and Wu (1994) found that these consumers rated their vocational skills, vocational motivation, and community living skills significantly higher than did their case managers. Sainfort, Becker, and Diamond (1996) found that consumers with chronic schizophrenia rated their social relationships and occupational situations better than did their providers. Correlations among consumers, family members, and providers were modest, suggesting a fair degree of uniqueness in the three perspectives. Although we need to know more about the validity of the perceptions of the different parties in consumers' environments, at least three self-report instruments are available.

A relative recent and somewhat unusual approach to assessing functioning is the Quality of Life Index for Mental Health (QLI-MH; Becker, Diamond, & Sainfort, 1993). This instrument was designed to be a consumer self-report approach, although comparable forms for providers and family members have also been developed. An interesting aspect of the QLI-MH is that a number of other, brief instruments were included in their totality as measures of various dimensions of quality of life (e.g., the Brief Psychiatric Rating Scale, described below) and as a measure of symptoms. The full instrument reportedly takes providers about 10 minutes to complete, and consumers 20–30 minutes. The QLI-MH scales of potential interest as measures of functioning and role performance are Occupational Activity, Social Relations, Economics, and Activities of Daily Living. One limitation of the instrument is a rather cumbersome scoring process. Although research has continued on the QLI-MH, there is not a great deal of information available about it. Although modest correlations have been reported between consumers and providers, which the authors interpret as suggesting construct validity, the correlations of .50–.55 suggest that consumers and providers have somewhat different views of consumers' quality of life. In spite of the obvious face validity of consumer self-descriptions on some dimensions, there may be circumstances and situations in which the consumers may have vested interests in outcome scores (e.g., eligibility for disability benefits) to demonstrate the lack of need for treatment or case management (also, see Massey & Wu, 1994). Although worth considering for outcome evaluation efforts, more research and experience with this approach and instrument are needed.

If self-report measures of consumer functioning and role performance are being seriously considered, the social functioning and role limitations due to emotional problems scales of the SF-36 (see above) should be considered (Ware et al., 1993). A significant advantage of these scales is the availability of public norms stratified by age and extensive psychometric information.

Sperry and his colleagues (1996) have described a 24-item self-report instrument called the Current Life Functioning scale. This instrument consists of six subscales: family, intimacy, social relationships, health and grooming, self-management, and work/school/household. The subscales have good internal reliability, but a couple of scales have dubious 3–4-week stability. The validity of the scales apparently have not been investigated, and nonconsumer norms are apparently not available.

SIGNIFICANT OTHER REPORTS OF CONSUMER FUNCTIONING AND ROLE PERFORMANCE

A seemingly little known and little used instrument, the Personal Adjustment and Role Skill scales (PARS; Ellsworth, 1975), is particularly appropriate in this domain (cell F, in Table 2, Chapter 4). The PARS was developed and tested specifically for use with consumers' significant others; that is, as a means for other people who know the consumer well to describe the consumers' adjustment and functioning. The instrument consists of nine scales, each consisting of three or four items. All of the scales have excellent internal consistency and reliability, and the instrument differentiates mental health clients and nonclients. Although there are scales that seek the significant other's perceptions of the consumer's depression, anxiety, substance use, and confusion, the scales particularly pertinent to functioning and role performance are household maintenance activities, employment/income, relationships with children (if present in the household), close relationships or interpersonal involvement, and outside social activities (outside of the home).

Because the scales are brief, they lend themselves to by-mail administration and inclusion with other brief measures. The issue of norms is complicated. General public or nonclient norms are not available. However, the author developed "change norms" that describe the average amount of change demonstrated by adult consumers over a 3-month period of treatment. These change scores are cumbersome to interpret to policy and funding personnel. The scales do have considerable "face" validity, and are useful for assessing pre- and posttreatment change. The close/interpersonal relationship and relations with children scales are among the few outcome-evaluation-friendly measures that attempt to assess relationships with others. An example of use of these scales is O'Sullivan and Speer's (1995) 2-year study of older adults with severe and persistent mental illness in a supported housing program.

Although developed to assist in assessment of older adults, an instrument to be considered for consumers with significant impairments is the Instrumental Activities of Daily Living Scale (IADL; Lawton & Brody, 1969). This is an eight-item scale evaluating a person's ability to perform everyday activities such as shopping, using a telephone, taking medications, and handling personal finances.

The IADL was designed to be used by others who know the consumer's functioning on a day-to-day basis. It has good interrater agreement and reliability. Although there are no general public norms, the items have face validity, and the scale has utility in assessing daily functioning over time. *Face validity* refers to items or questions the meaning and significance of which are so direct and obvious to the average layperson that extensive research is unnecessary to establish their meaning; examples include, Are you employed?, and Have you physically struck a person in your family during the past month? Speer (1993) used the IADL in a study of Parkinson's disease patients and caregivers adjustment over a 12-month period.

A somewhat different approach to assessing the consumer's functioning is examining the effects of his or her problems on a caregiving person. The Cost of Care Index (CCI; Kosberg, Cairl, & Keller, 1990) is one such instrument that assays the burden or price one has to pay socially, psychologically, and financially to provide care to a person with mental health problems. Although developed to evaluate the effects of dementing illnesses on care providers, burden has become increasingly a matter of concern to families of persons with severe mental illness. The CCI is a self-administering, 20-item questionnaire, with items rated on a four-point scale ranging from strongly agree to strongly disagree. Sample items are: I feel the patient is an overly demanding person to care for; I feel that caring for the patient puts a strain on family relationships; and I feel that caring for the patient interferes with my having friends or my family coming to my home. The CCI appears psychometrically sound.

If decision makers are concerned about family functioning, the Family Environment Scale (FES; Moos & Moos, 1981) is an excellent instrument to consider. The FES consists of 90 true–false items that constitute 10 scales. The FES has been extensively researched and has excellent reliability and validity. The usual approach to its use is to have several family members complete the questionnaire, and scoring consists of then determining the family's average raw score on the scales. Norms from over 1100 general public families are available. To me the scales with the greatest mental health service outcome potential are the family cohesion, expressiveness, and conflict scales (nine items in each scale). Through use of the norms, the family's deviance relative to general public families both before and after treatment can be determined. Henggler et al. (1992) used the FES in their study of community, family-oriented treatment of juvenile offenders.

A complication in the use of significant others as sources of outcome data is related to the right to privacy and the stigma of mental health problems and services. Many consumers, particularly outpatients, request services without their families knowledge. Many consumers do not want their families, neighbors, and employers to know that they are receiving treatment, and they may not provide the consent required for the significant others to be contacted.

PUBLIC GATEKEEPERS AS SOURCES OF DATA ABOUT CONSUMER FUNCTIONING AND ROLE PERFORMANCE

I am discussing here cell I in Table 2, from Chapter 4. Many of these measures have also been used as indices of quality of life. These kinds of information are usually not the result of standardized assessment procedures like those discussed above. In some instances the information is a matter of public record, subject to "Sunshine" laws. In other instances, confidentiality rules apply that require consumer permission to access data. Often, the sources of the data are civil servants or other community agency professionals who have contact with the consumers in the course of their jobs. In some instances, the consumers are the sources of the information, but the information is interpreted by the gate-keeper with respect to its veracity, or corroborating information is obtained informally from others such as family members. Such gatekeepers may be law-enforcement personnel, hospital staff (records), visiting nurses, public health clinic workers, welfare staff, child protection workers, Social Security records and staff, or they may be agencies or organizations. These types of information serve as indices or proxies for measures of how the consumer is functioning in the community, performing certain role behaviors, and complying with social rules and laws.

Perhaps the most global index of a consumer's overall functioning is whether or not he or she has been *hospitalized* during or after treatment for mental health or psychiatric reasons. This suggests that in somebody's view, including possibly the consumer's, that the consumer was in need of a restrictive level of professional care or oversight. Given the current urgency given to avoiding expensive inpatient care, the reasons for hospitalization are usually of a serious or emergency nature. A related kind of information is whether the hospitalization was voluntary or involuntary. Involuntary hospitalization implies a judgment that the person was a threat to him or herself or to someone else and unwilling to to seek treatment for the underlying condition. In this sense, voluntary entry to inpatient care may suggest a higher level of awareness and functioning than an involuntary admission. Days of hospitalization during a given time period such as a year, or as a proportion of pretreatment days of hospitalization, are common indices of extent of inpatient care. Examples of studies using hospitalization data as outcome measures include Bigelow, McFarland, Gareau, and Young's (1991) study of intensive community services for former state hospital patients; Brown, Ridgeway, Anthony, and Rogers (1991) study of involuntary assignment of young adults with chronic mental illness to supported housing services; and Hiday and Scheid-Cook's (1989) study of adults with chronic mental illness who were involuntarily committed to outpatient treatment.

An obvious complication is that receiving mental health or psychiatric treatment is a sensitive matter, subject to many rules and regulations regarding consumers' rights to privacy and requiring consumer consent to divulge the information. If the consumer is still in ambulatory treatment or receiving follow-up or case management services, this may facilitate obtaining hospitalization information. Usually, however, some form of prospective action will be required of the evaluating entity that provides the consumer's permission for follow-up contact and/or obtaining information from other providers.

An index of conformity or compliance with laws as an estimate of community functioning are variables related to *incarceration and arrests*. These outcome variables may be most relevant for programs serving consumers with severe alcohol and/or drug problems. Another group of pertinent consumers are those with violence-control difficulties, such as spouse and child abusers. Number of arrests, or days of incarceration, during or after having received mental health or substance abuse services have been used as outcome variables. Also, the type of alleged crime, such as a violent or sexual assault crime, may be an important outcome variable. The major limitation of arrests as an outcome is that so few crimes (perhaps 10–20%) result in arrests and convictions. An asymmetry exists: if an arrest occurs, noncompliance with social rules has probably occurred; if no arrests occur, the consumer may or may not have complied with the law. Examples of use of these kinds of variables include Marques, Day, Nelson, and West's (1994) study of the effectiveness of intensive inpatient cognitive behavioral treatment of adult sex offenders, and Peters, Kearns, Murrin, Dolente, and May's (1993) study of the outcomes of jail-based, cognitive behavioral, and relapse-prevention treatment of substance-abusing jail inmates. With the exception of juveniles, this type of information is usually a matter of public record and thus relatively easily obtainable.

A rather major and basic kind of role performance measure is the person's ability to support themselves financially. Employment is the usual index here. Although employment and adequacy of income are most often investigated in programs serving seriously and persistently mentally ill consumers, current business conditions, downsizing, and layoffs suggest that employment may be an important outcome variable in emergency, domestic violence, and family problem service programs. Although these data often come through a community gatekeeper, the source is usually the consumer. Often, the information is readily subject to confirmation by family members or others who know the consumer. Because of the stagnation of incomes in the population, when reemployment occurs the income differential between prior and new employment may be an important measure and possibly suggestive of incipient stress even though the consumer is now "employed." Studies of use of employment and income as outcome variables include Caton, Wyatt, Grunberg, and Felix's (1990) study of on-site mental health day treatment for homeless mentally ill men in a homeless shelter; Cook, Graham, and Razzano's (1993) study of residential, re-habilitation and intensive case management services for deaf and mentally ill adults; and Leda and Rosenheck's (1992) study of intensive medical, psychiatric, rehabilitation, and substance abuse treatment in a domicillary program for homeless mentally ill veterans.

Housing and quality of the home are additional important and basic outcome matters. The supported housing movement, stimulated by consumers and consumer advocate groups have called attention to the deficiencies and limitations of professionally managed housing, such as residential treatment and half-way house programs. Matters of privacy, independence, the absence of professionals and other consumers, and quality of housing have become urgent for consumers and gradually for public funders of support services for consumers. The first question, obviously, is whether or not the consumer has a home or is homeless. For consumers with a history of homelessness, number of days homeless have been used as an outcome variable. A second matter is whether or not the home is some form of supervised or sheltered residence, or is it a home that exists in the open housing market. The quality of the neighborhood and safety are additional considerations. The physical quality of the residence (e.g., peeling paint, broken windows, plumbing, heating, etc.) is obviously a related variable that can strongly affect a person's morale. These variables are often subsumed under the broader rubric of quality of life. Studies examining the use of housing variables as outcome variables include Morse, Calsyn, Allen, Tempelhoff, and Smith's (1992) study of the effectiveness of assertive outreach and intensive case management relative to a daytime drop-in center and routine outpatient treatment for homeless consumers with mental illness; Bigelow et al. (1991) study of intensive community services for former state hospital residents; and Bybee, Mowbray, and Cohen's (1995) study of outreach, linkage, advocacy, and case management services for homeless adults with mental illness.

A final functioning and role performance group of measures are those involving self-care or self-maintenance. Dimensions here include such things as personal hygiene, cleanliness, care of clothing, cooking, nutrition, and occasionally include such things as capability for making and keeping medical appointments and being responsible for taking medications. The two ultimate goals here are health maintenance and appearence in the service of social relationships. Consumers for whom these may be pertinent issues include severely depressed persons, people with severe psychotic or developmentally disabling conditions, and people who are homeless. Gatekeepers who are often aware of and capable of assessing these variables include visiting nurses, anyone making home visits, intensive case managers, and health-care workers. The Bigelow et al. (1991) study and the Hiday and Scheid-Cook (1989) study cited above are examples of studies assessing this category of outcome variables.

SYMPTOMS AND DISORDERS ASSESSED BY INDEPENDENT OBSERVERS, THERAPISTS, OR MENTAL HEALTH SERVICE PROVIDERS

The two categories of variables by data sources, cells **K** and **N** in Table 2, Chapter 4, will be discussed together because the assessment instruments can be employed either by independent observers or provider clinicians. The first two instruments are both interview-based techniques that presuppose significant clinical experience and expertise.

One of the most widely used traditional clinician interview- based symptom measures is the Hamilton Rating Scale for Depression (HRSD; Hamilton, 1960). The scale includes items assessing such symptom components as feelings of guilt, suicidal ideation, insomnia, gastrointestinal symptoms, and weight loss. Part of the popularity of this 24-item scale in treatment and drug research is that the various rating points for each item are relativly well defined in behavioral terms. Ordinarily, this scale is used in the context of a psychiatric or clinical diagnostic interview. The HRSD has been used in research in which both provider clinicians and independent interviewers have provided the ratings. Although the instrument has a strong tradition in psychiatric research, it does presuppose some clinical experience and sophistication, and, to my knowledge, does not have nonpatient norms available.

Another widely used instrument with a long tradition in psychiatric research and outcome evaluation is the Brief Psychiatric Rating Scale (BPRS; Overall & Gorham, 1962). This instrument consists of 18 seven-point ratings scales with the rating points ranging from not present to extremely severe. Sample scales are emotional withdrawal, conceptual disorganization, grandiosity, hallucinatory behavior, and blunted affect. The purpose of this technique is to quantify the major components of a psychiatric evaluation. Again, there do not appear to be public norms available, but the BPRS has been used and can be used in pretreatment–posttreatment assessment situations to examine change in dimensions of psychopathology. Whether or not this kind of data would be of interest or use to policy and administrative decision makers is somewhat doubtful.

The history of dubious reliability and poor interrater agreement of psychiatric diagnoses has led to the evolution of at least two structured diagnostic interview instruments keyed to the Diagnostic and Statistical Manuals of Mental Disorders (APA, 1994). These structured interview instruments have resulted in much more reliable diagnoses to the point where they have often been required for federally funded clinical and services research. Both of the instruments cited here require significant training and practice, and one requires a fair amount of clinical experience and expertise. After the training, each consumer interview may take 1–2 hours, although computerized and short forms are beginning to appear on the market.

The oldest and most extensively researched instrument is the Diagnostic Interview Schedule (DIS), which was commissioned by the National Institute of Mental Health (NIMH), and was the basic instrument used in the national Epidemiologic Catchment Area Study (e.g., Robins et al., 1984). The DIS, updates, training materials, and various adaptations of the DIS are available from the Washington University School of Medicine, Department of Psychiatry, (4940 Children's Place, St. Louis, MO 63110). As indicated above, the very specific interview questions, prompts, and decision instructions and rules in the DIS result in psychiatric diagnoses with higher reliabilities than earlier nonstructured clinical diagnoses.

The second and more recently developed structured diagnostic instrument is the Structured Clinical Interview for *DSM-III-R* (SCID; Spitzer, Williams, Gibbon, & First, 1989). Like the DIS, the SCID is a highly structured interview technique that produces psychiatric diagnoses. The SCID permits more latitude and departures from the structured format to seek further clinically indicated clarification and information. Because of this, a weakness of the SCID is that more training, experience, and sophistication on the part of the interviewer is required than is presupposed by the DIS.

An early disadvantage of the DIS was that it investigated only one personality disorder, Antisocial Personality Disorder. Initially the SCID permitted exploration of a broader range of Axis II disorders. However, subsequent development of the DIS remedied this limitation. The earlier forms of both instruments were costly and time consuming because of the training required and the necessity of almost full-spectrum psychiatric interviews. More recent research with abbreviated forms may have alleviated these problems somewhat. Also, the utility of diagnostic information for policy makers remains to be seen.

An example of the use of diagnosis as an outcome measure is provided by the NIMH Treatment of Depression Collaborative Research Program (Elkin, 1994). The HRSD and the SCL-90, among others, were the primary outcome variables at the end of treatment in this multisite study of short-term structured individual psychotherapy for outpatients with major depressive Disorder. During the 18-month posttreatment follow-up phase of the study, continued remission from or reoccurrence of major depression was studied (a variant of a structured clinical interview technique was used; Shea et al., 1992). This study suggests that the use of a diagnosable disorder as an outcome criterion may be a very stringent test of treatment effectiveness.

FUNCTIONING AND ROLE PERFORMANCE ASSESSED BY INDEPENDENT OBSERVERS

Probably the most common approach to the assessment of consumer functioning in psychiatric research and service evaluation, particularly among consumers who are severely and persistently mentally ill, is via independent interviewers. The broad Quality of Life construct has become the most recent politically correct concept in community support services evaluation. The popularity of the concept has led to a recent flood of interview-based instruments that assess various aspects of daily functioning and role performance, many under the rubric of quality of life, for example, Satisfaction with Life Domains Scale (Calsyn, Morse, Tempelhoff, Smith, & Allen, 1995), the Role Functioning Scale (Goodman, Sewell, Cooley, & Leavitt, 1993), and the California Adult Performance Outcome Survey (Cuffel et al., 1995).

The method with the longest history and greatest development and refinement is the Lehman Quality of Life Interview (LQOLI; Lehman, Kernan, & Postrado, no date; Lehman, 1988). This instrument comes in two forms: the Full form consists of 158 items and takes about 45 minutes to complete; the Brief version consists of 78 items and takes about 15 minutes for a trained interviewer to complete. The LQOLI does not require clinical training and experience, but does require training in use of the instrument, supervision, and practice. The authors recommend practice and supervision until there is 80% agreement between the trainee and the expert supervisor. The dimensions of the LQOLI most pertinent to role performance are Living Situation, Daily Activities and Functioning, Social Relations, Finances, Work and School, and Legal and Safety Issues. Reliability and validity information is based on data from over 1800 individuals with severe and persistent mental illness, in four studies over a 13-year period. The instrument has excellent internal reliability and scale independence and reasonable validity. A weakness of any consumer interview-based method, relative to information from significant others for example, is that the interviewer does not observe the consumer in his or her natural environment and circumstances as would a family member. The interviewer, however, would not be subject to concern about vested interests in the service program or provider agency. An example of the use of the instrument in outcome evaluation is Lehman et al. (1994) study of the effects of reorganization and integration of case management services among over 600 consumers with chronic mental illness in the community.

FUNCTIONING AND ROLE PERFORMANCE ASSESSED BY PROVIDERS

Another relatively recent instrument designed to assess role performance among consumers with mental illness in the community is a series of functioning scales based on the Missouri Levels of Care instrument (Kramer, Massey, & Pokorny, 1990; Massey & Wu, 1994). This instrument was designed specifically to be used by case managers, although data from consumers and family members are also available. The instrument consists of 63 items that comprise eight scales pertinent to the community functioning of adults with mental illness: vocational skills, vocational motivation, community living skills, self-care, nuisance behaviors, sociability, violence, and irritability. This approach has been used to profile consumers appropriate for different types of community placements.

The eight scales have generally good reliability when completed by case managers, consumers, and family members. The scales have good face and empirical validity. An interesting study using this instrument provided suggestive information about agreement among the three groups. Although there were statistically significant correlations among the three groups, the degree of correlation was very modest, suggesting again that the different groups have moderately distinct perspectives. Interestingly, the best agreement was between case managers and family members. Futhermore, case managers rated the consumers *lower* on vocational skills and motivation and living skills than did the consumers (Massey & Wu, 1994). We will return to the matter of potential biases in different perspectives again in the next chapter.

Although I share with some important stakeholders some uneasiness about providers as sources of outcome data, in this domain I am inclined to do an about-face. Case managers, particularly those in intensive case management programs with their usually strong commitments to consumers, may be less subject to the vested interest bias favoring their parent organization than other types of providers. In addition, case managers who provide their services in vivo will generally know the full gamut of consumer skills and behavior better than office-based clinicians (i.e., they will have more firsthand knowledge). The ideal situation is that relatively rare circumstance where the agency providing case management is different or separate from the agency providing treatment services. In this instance, the case managers approximate independent observers except that they are likely to have more direct information.

GOAL ATTAINMENT SCALING: A GENERIC APPROACH

The decades-old debate about the appropriateness of standardized measures that are used for all consumers (nomothetic) versus consumer-specific measures (idiographic) as outcome measures, simply will not go away (e.g., Nelson-Gray, 1996). All of the measures discussed thus far have been of the former type. We would be remiss, however, not to mention a prominent method for creating outcome measures that are specific to individual consumers and which differ among consumers, Goal Attainment Scaling (GAS; Kiresuk, 1973). The criticism of standardized measures is that because all consumers are different their problems and the criteria for their successful treatment should be different.

From this standpoint, use of standardized measures ignore these differences and force all consumers into the same mold with respect to evaluating the outcomes of the services they receive.

To address this concern, Kiresuk and his colleagues developed a method for creating treatment goal scales that would be unique for each individual consumer. Several goals are identified in collaboration with the consumer at admission, and five behaviorally defined levels of attainment are then written for each goal scale, with the middle level being the expected attainment within 3 months. The consumer may score at the expected level, better than expected or worse than expected, after 3 months. The goals may involve distress reduction, changes in role performance, relationships with others, functioning, or anything pertinent to the consumer's adjustment; it is a truly generic approach. Kiresuk also developed a companion statistical process for converting the attainment scores into standard scores so that a score of 50 represents "expected" goal attainment for all consumers. Ideally, the initial goal scales are written, and they are scored 3 months later, by someone different than the therapist treating the consumer. If the consumer remains in treatment beyond 3 months, the process is repeated for the second 3-month period. This is a creative integration of management, tracking, and evaluation of the treatment process.

During the 1970s and early 1980s, a lot of development work and research was conducted using the GAS. This work revealed three primary difficulties with GAS. In order for the process to be standard across all intake writers and follow-up scorers, considerable training and practice were required. The process also proved to be very time consuming and, thus, expensive. Finally, the data generated by the method proved difficult to interpret to policy and decision makers (e.g., "Specifically, what does 'expected goal achievement' for these 83 clients mean?"). Summarized and easily comprehended data have great appeal to decision makers.

Nonetheless, the clinical and treatment relevance of the method contributes to its resilience. Developments in recent years have turned toward introducing some standardization into the originally unstandardized approach. This has taken the form of creating a menu of, for example, 25–30 goal topics common to a particular service population, selecting the four to six most pertinent for an individual consumer, and then slightly modifying the levels for each consumer as needed. An example of this approach is provided by Schalock, Sheehan, and Weber (1993) in a state hospital admissions ward with a mean length of stay of 3 weeks. Here the goals were short-term and monitored and scored on a weekly basis. Consumers who relapsed and those who did not differed significantly in their in-hospital goal attainment in the expected direction.

Although GAS in its original and traditional form does not seem cost efficient for large-scale programs that may serve large numbers of consumers for short periods, it is worthy of consideration for programs providing costly, intensive services for a relatively small number of consumers over longer time periods (e.g., day treatment, residential treatment or halfway house programs). The problem of interpreting results to policy makers may remain, however.

In summary, a number of measuring instruments that I am familiar with have been described, along with their relative strengths and weaknesses. Self-administering measures of distress and symptoms are recommended for assessing consumer pain and distress, as are significant others, public gatekeepers, independent interviewers and case managers as sources of information about consumer functioning and role performance. If psychiatric disorders and psychopathology are relevant for policy and decision makers, independent interviewers and provider clinicians are the best sources of information.

REFERENCES

APA (1994). *Diagnostic and statistical manual of mental disorders* (4th ed.). Washington, DC: American Psychiatric Association.

Becker, M., Diamond, R., & Sainfort, F. (1993). A new patient-focused index for measuring quality of life in persons with severe and persistent mental illness. *Quality of Life Research, 2,* 239–251.

Bigelow, D. A., McFarland, B. H., Gareau, M. J., & Young, D. J. (1991). Implementation and effectiveness of a bed reduction project. *Community Mental Health Journal, 27,* 125–133.

Brown, M. A., Ridgway, P., Anthony, W. A., & Rogers, E. S. (1991). Comparison of outcomes for clients seeking and assigned to supported housing. *Hospital and Community Psychiatry, 42,* 1150–1153.

Burke, W. J., Roccaforte, W. H., Wengel, S. P., Conley, D. M., & Potter, J. F. (1995). The reliability and validity of the Geriatric Depression Rating Scale administered by telephone. *Journal of the American Geriatrics Society, 43,* 674–679.

Bybee, D., Mowbray, C. T., & Cohen, E. H. (1995). Evaluation of a homeless mentally ill outreach program: Differential short-term effects. *Evaluation and Program Planning, 18,* 13–24.

Calsyn, R. J., Morse, G. A., Tempelhoff, B., Smith, R., & Allen, G. (1995). Homeless mentally ill clients and the quality of life. *Evaluation and Program Planning, 18,* 219–225.

Caton, C. L. M., Wyatt, R. J., Grunberg, J., & Felix, A. (1990). An evaluation of a mental health program for homeless men. *American Journal of Psychiatry, 147,* 286–289.

Cohen, S., Mermelstein, R., Kamarck, T., & Hoberman, H. M. (1985). Measuring the functional components of social support. In I. G. Sarason & B. R. Sarason (Eds.), *Social support: Theory, research and applications* (pp. 73–94). Boston: Dordrecht.

Cohen, S. & Williamson, G. (1988). Perceived stress in a probability sample of the United States. In S. Spacapan & S. Oskamp (Eds.), *The Social Psychology of Health: Claremont Symposium on Applied Psychology* (pp. 31–68). Newbury Park, CA: Sage.

Conoley, J. C., & Impara, J. C. (1995). *The Twelfth Mental Measurement Yearbook.* Lincoln, NE: The University of Nebraska-Lincoln.

Cook, J. A., Graham, K. K., & Razzano, L. (1993). Psychosocial rehabilitation of deaf persons with severe mental illness: A multivariate model of residential outcomes. *Rehabilitation Psychology, 38,* 261–274.

Cuffel, B. J., Snowden, L., Green, R. S., McConnell, W., Mandella, V., & Styc, K. (1995). The California adult performance outcome survey: Preliminary evidence on reliability and validity. *Community Mental Health Journal, 31,* 425–436.

Dupuy, H. J. (1977). *A concurrent validational study of the NCHS general well-being schedule.* (DHEW Publication No. HRA 78-1347). Hyattsville, MD: National Center for Health Statistics, U.S. Department of Health, Education, and Welfare.

Elkin, I. (1994). The NIMH treatment of depression collaborative research program: Where we began and where we are. In A. E. Bergin & S. L. Garfield (Eds.), *Handbook of psychotherapy and behavior change* (pp. 114–140). New York: John Wiley & Sons.

Ellsworth, R. B. (1975). Consumer feedback in measuring the effectiveness of mental health programs. In M. Guttentag & E. L. Struennig (Eds.), *Handbook of evaluation research* (Vol. 2, pp. 239–274). Beverly Hills: Sage.

Goodman, S. H., Sewell, D. R., Cooley, E. L., & Leavitt, N. (1993). Assessing levels of adaptive functioning: The role functioning scale. *Community Mental Health Journal, 29,* 119–31.

Graham, J. R. (1990). *MMPI-2: Assessing personality and psychopathology.* New York: Oxford University Press.

Hamilton, M. A. (1960). A rating scale for depression. *Journal of Neurological and Neurosurgical Psychiatry, 25,* 56–62.

Henggeler, S. W., Melton, G. B., & Smith, L. A. (1992). Family preservation using multisystemic therapy: An effective alternative to incarcerating serious juvenile offenders. *Journal of Consulting and Clinical Psychology, 60,* 953–961.

Hiday, V. A., & Scheid-Cook, T. L. (1989). A follow-up of chronic patients committed to outpatient treatment. *Hospital and Community Psychiatry, 40,* 52–59.

Kiresuk, T. J. (1973). Goal Attainment Scaling at a county mental health service. *Evaluation,* (No. 1), 12–18.

Kosberg, J. I., Cairl, R. E., & Keller, D. M. (1990). Components of burden: Interventive implications. *The Gerontologist, 30,* 236–242.

Kramer, H. B., Massey, O. T., & Pokorny, L. J. (1990). Development and validation of a level-of-care instrument for predicting residential placement. *Hospital and Community Psychiatry, 41,* 407–412.

Lawton, M. P., & Brody, E. M. (1969). Assessment of older people: Self-maintaining and instrumental activities of daily living. *Gerontologist, 9,* 179–186.

Leda, C., & Rosenheck, R. (1992). Mental health status and community adjustment after treatment in a residential treatment program for homeless veterans. *American Journal of Psychiatry, 149,* 1219–1224.

Lehman, A. F. (1988). A quality of life interview for the chronically mentally ill. *Evaluation and Program Planning, 11,* 51–62.

Lehman, A., Kernan, E., & Postrado, L. (no date). *Toolkit for evaluating quality of life for persons with severe mental illness.* Baltimore: Center for Mental Health Services Research, University of Maryland School of Medicine.

Lehman, A. E., Postrado, L. T., Roth, D., McNary, S. W., & Goldman, H. H. (1994). Continuity of care and client outcomes in the Robert Wood Johnson Foundation program on chronic mental illness. *Milband Quarterly, 72,* 105–122.

Marques, J. K., Day, D. M., Nelson, C., & West, M. A. (1994). Effects of cognitive-behavioral treatment on sex offender recidivism: Preliminary results of a longitudinal study. *Criminal Justice and Behavior, 21,* 28–54.

Massey, O. T., & Wu, L. (1994). Three critical views of functioning: Comparisons of assessments made by individuals with mental illness, their case managers, and family members. *Evaluation and Program Planning, 17,* 1–7.

Moos, R. H., & Moos, B. S. (1981). *Family Environment Scale Manual.* Palo Alto, CA: Consulting Psychologists Press.

Morishita, L., Boult, C., Ebbitt, B., Rambel, M., Fallstrom, K., & Gooden, T. (1995). Concurrent validity of administering the Geriatric Depression Scale and the Physical Functioning dimension of the SIP by telephone. *Journal of the American Geriatrics Society, 43,* 680–683.

Morse, G. A., Calsyn, R. J., Allen, G., Tempelhoff, B., & Smith, R. (1992). Experimental comparison of the effects of three treatment programs for homeless mentally ill people. *Hospital and Community Psychiatry, 43,* 1005–1010.

Nelson-Gray, R. O. (1996). Treatment outcome measures: Nomothetic or idiographic? *Clinical Psychology: Science and Practice, 3,* 164–167.

O'Sullivan, M., & Speer, D. (1995). *The supported housing Program, Broward County elderly services, Ft. Lauderdale, FL: Evaluation final report.* Tampa, FL: de la Parte Florida Mental Health Instituite.

Overall, J. E., & Gorham, D. R. (1962). The Brief Psychiatric Rating Scale. *Psychological Reports, 10,* 799–812.

Parmelee, P. A., & Katz, I. R. (1990). Geriatric Depression Scale. *Journal of the American Geriatrics Society, 38,* 1379.

Peters, R. A., Kearns, W. D., Murrin, M. R., Dolente, A. S., & May, R. L. (1993). Examining the effectiveness of in-jail substance abuse treatment. *Journal of Offender Rehabilitation, 19,* 1–39.

Procidano, M. E., & Heller, K. (1983). Measures of perceived social support from friends and from family: Three validation studies. *American Journal of Community Psychology, 11,* 1–24.

Radloff, L. S. (1977). The CES-D scale: A self-report depression scale for research in the general population. *Applied Psychological Measurement, 1,* 385–401.

Robins, L. N., Helzer, J. E., Weissman, M. M., Orvaschel, H., Gruenberg, E., Burke, J. D., & Regier, D. A. (1984). Lifetime prevalence of specific psychiatric disorders in three sites. *Archives of General Psychiatry, 41,* 949–958.

Riggio, R. E. (1986). Assessment of basic social skills. *Journal of Personality and Social Psychology, 51,* 649–660.

Sainfort, F., Becker, M., & Diamond, R. (1996). Judgments of quality of life of individuals with severe mental disorders: Patient self-report versus provider perspectives. *American Journal of Psychiatry, 153,* 497–502.

Schalock, R. L., Sheehan, M. J., & Weber, L. (1993). The use of treatment progress scales in client monitoring and evaluation. *The Journal of Mental Health Admiminstration, 20,* 264–269.

Sederer, L. I., & Dickey, B. (1996). *Outcomes assessment in clinical practice.* Baltimore: Williams & Wilkins.

Shea, M. T., Ilkin, I., Imber, S. D., Sotsky, S. M., Watkins, J. T. Collins, J. F., Pilkonis, P. A., Beckham, E., Glass, D. R., Dolan, R. T., & Parloff, M. B. (1992). Course of depressive symptoms over follow-up: Findings from the National Insitute of Mental Health Treatment of Depression Collaborative Research Program. *Archives of General Psychiatry, 49,* 782–787.

Sheikh, J. I., & Yesavage, J. A. (1986). Geriatric Depression Scale (GDS): Recent evidence and development of a shorter form. In T. L. Brink (Ed.), *Clinical gerontology: A guide to assessment and intervention* (pp. 165–174). New York: Haworth Press.

Smith, V. L. (1996). Symptom Checklist-90-Revised (SCL-90-R) and the Brief Symptom Inventory (BSI). In L. I. Sederer & B. Dickey (Eds.), *Outcomes assessment in clinical practice* (pp. 89–91). Baltimore: Williams & Wilkins.

Speer, D. C. (1993). Predicting Parkinson's Disease patient and caregiver adjustment: Preliminary findings. *Behavior, Health and Aging, 3,* 139–146.

Speer, D. C. (1994). Can treatment research inform decision makers? Nonexperimental method issues and examples among older outpatients. *Journal of Consulting and Clinical Psychology, 62,* 560–568.

Speer, D. C., & Swindle, R. (1982). The "monitoring model" and the mortality X treatment interaction threat to validity in mental health outcome evaluation. *American Journal of Community Psychology, 10,* 541–552.

Sperry, L., Brill, P. L., Howard, K. I., & Grissom, G. R. (1996). *Treatment outcomes in psychotherapy and psychiatric interventions.* New York: Brunner/Mazel.

Spitzer, R. L., Williams, J. B. W., Gibbon, M., & First, M. B. (1989). *Instruction Manual for the Structured Clinical Interview for DSM-III-R: SCID.* New York: Biometrics Research.

The 1996 Behavioral Outcomes & Guidelines Sourcebook (1995). New York: Faulkner & Gray, Inc.

Ware, J. E., Kosinski, M., & Keller, S. D. (1994). *SF-36 physical and mental component summary measures—A user's manual.* Boston: New England Medical Center, The Health Institute.

Ware, J. E., & Sherbourne, C. D. (1992). The MOS 36-item short-form health survey (SF-36). *Medical Care, 30,* 473–481.

Ware, J. E., Snow, K. K., Kosinski, M., & Gandek, B. (1993). *SF-36 health survey manual and interpretation guide.* Boston: New England Medical Center, The Health Institute.

Yesavage, J., & Brink, T. L. (1983). Development and validation of a geriatric depression scale: A preliminary report. *Journal of Psychiatric Research, 17,* 37–49.

CHAPTER 6

Potential Booby Traps and Landmines

The purpose of this chapter is to alert the reader to some sources of risk of drawing misleading conclusions. Some traps or landmines may lead to exaggerated or unduly optimistic views about the effectiveness of services, whereas others may lead to an underestimation of service effectiveness. We are here confronting the tension and strain between the rigor of the scientific approach and the greater uncertainty and feasibility issues of program evaluation.

In technical parlance, the issue is *bias* that may be introduced into the data by various aspects of the design of the evaluation or data collection. Bias is the systematic slanting of data in one way or another so that results are not representative of all people in the group being studied. Ordinarily, psychosocial research assumes that the inevitable errors related to measurement or data collection are random, and that they cancel each other out. Bias occurs when errors systematically occur in one direction so that canceling does not occur. These systematically accumulating errors may then lead to distorted or misleading conclusions by the unwary evaluator.

After declaring that in outcome evaluation we need to trade some rigor and certainty for feasibility and relevance, I may appear guilty of double-speak. Generally, the principle that some outcome data are better than no outcome data is useful, *as long as the evaluator is aware of possible distortions or biases in the data and qualifies inferences and conclusions accordingly.* Drawing fair and reasonable conclusions is neither simple nor uncomplicated; in some ways experimental research is more straightforward because one simply has to follow methodological rules. Program evaluation, on the other hand, may require more awareness, judgment, and professional responsibility in interpreting the numbers and drawing conclusions than does highly contolled scientific research.

The ultimate principle proposed here is that within the constraints of feasibility and relevance, the evaluator should strive to minimize systematic distortions in the data and be sensitive to the possible need to qualify conclusions in light of distortions that may affect the veracity of those conclusions. This sensitivity, however, presupposes an awareness of what are some of the pertinent booby traps.

"VESTED INTERESTS" AND PROVIDER RATINGS

Perhaps one of the most controversial and complicated potential sources of bias or distortion is outcome-rating data provided by the service providers. This is a variation of the conflict-of-interest situation, in which the sources of the information have a stake or interest in the conclusions drawn from the information (i.e., the results may have consequences for the sources of the data). This is also a situation in which the *appearance* or suspicion of conflict of interest may be as damaging to the credibility of the conclusions as the potential bias introduced by the sources of the data.

Part of the complexity of this matter, and part of its attractiveness as a source of information about consumer outcomes, is that provider ratings of client adjustment *solve a different potential source of bias*—that of potential bias introduced by data loss and consumer attrition from the study cohort. When a sizable proportion of consumers in the evaluation study refuse to participate or cannot be located, the remaining members of the group tend to be unrepresentative of consumers designated to be in the original cohort and in the program in general. However, service providers are under the administrative influence of the agency whose program is being evaluated. Theoretically, the agency has the administrative leverage to obtain ratings from providers for 100% of the consumers in the evaluation cohort. This potentially solves the problem of unrepresentativeness of the remaining cohort introduced by consumer self-selection or nonparticipation. Obviously, this strategy has a lot of appeal. Another appealing aspect is that providing the ratings can be included in providers' job responsibilities, thus minimizing the costs of data collection.

The downside of using provider ratings as outcome or response to treatment measures is the possible suspicion by policy makers that providers will be tempted to "gild the lily" when an evaluation of their own service program is involved. One need not assume that providers are dishonest, or will falsify data, for this to be a reasonable concern. Providers are first of all human beings, and most human beings like to think of themselves and be perceived by others as doing a good job. In a real sense, providers are being asked, perhaps unreasonably, to evaluate their own work—although the outcome evaluation effort is usually not described in these terms. It is a natural and normal human tendency, when in doubt or when the consumer's adjustment is unclear, to give the consumer and thereby *the provider* the benefit of the doubt. That is, when a significant period of time has elapsed or when the provider does not have information about a particular aspect of the client's adjustment, the provider may be inclined to rate the consumer as better adjusted than someone else with more direct or more current information might rate the consumer.

It is also worth noting that when the stakes or consequences for the provider agency increase, the implicit and unintentional pressure on providers to "gild the lily" may also increase. For example, if the provider agency's funding or contract for the following year is in some way contingent on agency "performance" as assessed by provider outcome ratings, it would be reasonable to think that the providers' states of mind vis-à-vis the contingency and the ratings will be affected. Provider generosity in giving the consumers (and therefore the providers) the benefit of the doubt may also inadvertently increase under these circumstances.

Another disadvantage of provider ratings is that clinicians dislike doing the ratings and often experience the process as burdensome. The aversiveness of this responsibility is not without basis. Recent years have witnessed an explosion in the amount of paperwork, forms, and records that are demanded of clinicians who are also expected to serve more and more consumers every week. Clinician time is not without cost.

A further difficulty arises if outcome information from different programs, provider organizations, or geographic areas are to be compared. Because provider rating instruments are rarely standardized, we usually do not know if providers in different organizations or areas are using the same frame of reference, if they are interpreting the rating items in the same way, or if they are evaluating change in the same way. Thus, if differences emerge between different provider organizations, or organizations in different areas, it is usually difficult to determine whether the differences tell us about the consumers receiving services or reflect variations in how the providers conducted the rating process.

The previously cited outcome evaluation of the effects of mental health services to nursing home residents conducted by my colleagues and I provide examples of these difficulties (Speer, O'Sullivan, & Lester, 1996). The mental health services were provided by two separate organizations in two different geographic areas and by two different groups of providers. The only feasible source of outcome data was the providers themselves. The providers were asked to rate the severity of residents' referral problems at admission and at a subsequent point in time. The providers were obviously aware that the program was being evaluated, and how the program was to be funded in the future was not clear. Furthermore, some of the outcome data at different points in time suggested that nursing home consumers served by one organization improved more than did the residents served by the other organization. Was the one organization more effective than the other, or did the different providers go about rating the consumers differently?

The primary justifications for conducting the evaluation under these circumstances were (a) an evaluation plan was mandated by the funding source; (b) the investigators were not aware of any other attempts to evaluate the outcomes of mental health services to nursing home residents; and (c) the report emphasized that the findings were from the *providers'* point of view and that the data may have been subject to vested interest influences. This study was viewed largely as a starting point for future outcome evaluations among nursing home residents. However, it also exemplifies the complications introduced by policy makers and program directors who mandate but do not fund evaluation studies. But, with responsible reporting some outcome data are better than no outcome data. . . . At a minimum, such potentially vulnerable data may provide a counterpoint that stimulates more robust future evaluations.

There is some empirical evidence suggesting that there may be substance to the concern about the effects of provider-vested interest on provider ratings. In a review of the sensitivity to change of different kinds of measurement techniques in psychotherapy research, Lambert and Hill (1994) concluded that therapist-based data suggest greater change, or improvement, than do data from consumer self-reports, significant others, and institutional records. Data reported by Nicholson (1989) exemplify the dilemma. In a follow-up evaluation of the outpatient treatment of 241 adolescents, she compared the ratings provided by parents with those provided by therapists. The parents of 21% of the teenage clients indicated that the referral problem was "completely better," whereas the therapists of 42% of the young people rated the referral problems as "completely resolved"; the "completely better" rate of the therapists was twice that of the parents. One of the earliest studies of this phenomenon was conducted by Lambert, Hatch, Kingston, and Edwards (1986) using meta-analytic technology. They found that consumer ratings of their own depression on two self-report scales (the Zung and the Beck depression scales) indicated significantly less change than did the ratings by providers using the Hamilton Rating Scale for Depression (HRSD).

I observed what I considered an example of the intrusion of extraneous therapist variables into the rating process in a pilot study. The pilot investigation involved goal-attainment scales created and subsequently scored by outpatient therapists. Each therapist scored the goal attainment of 5–6 of his or her own clients. Because I was supervising two of the therapists, I knew them and their clients well. Both therapists were competent and honest. However, one consistently rated all of his or her clients as having achieved very little goal attainment, whereas the other therapist consistently rated all his or her clients as having accomplished very high goal attainment. I believe that the dramatic differences had more to do with therapists' personality differences than with consumers' responses to treatment.

The provider ratings as outcome measures issue is usually discussed from the standpoint that therapists may provide more optimistic or favorable ratings of change than do the consumers or significant others who know the consumers well. In this context, the concern is that conclusions based on therapist data will suggest more effective services than are really the case. An alternative conceptual framework, broached in Chapter 4 on measurement, is that the different observers (e.g., the client, the therapist, and significant others) simply have different moderately unique perspectives. From this perspective, no single observational point of view is absolutely more valid than any other in a broad general sense. Each point of view may, however, have an intrinsically valid perspective on some unique aspect of the consumers' overall adjustment. The consumer is with him or herself all the time; the provider observes the consumer largely in treatment or rehabilitation settings in which he or she is being confronted and is expected to deal with change issues; significant others observe the consumer at home and in the community as he or she struggles to cope with and adapt to the demands of community life (intensive case managers may also fall into this latter category). A number of studies have produced statistically significant but modest correlations between different types of observers (e.g., Becker, Diamond, & Sainfort, 1993; Massey & Wu, 1994). Rather than indicating modest concurrent validity, these findings may simply reflect the uniqueness of the different perspectives of the consumers' adjustment in different circumstances with differing demands and expectations. As the old story about the blind men and the elephant suggests, all the perspectives may be valid, just different. From the standpoint of mental health policy and decision makers, the question reduces to which perspective is of most interest and value to the decision makers.

The use of provider ratings as outcome measures is especially relevant at the time of this writing because several states are developing statewide outcome evaluation systems based on provider ratings. This is particularly intriguing because some legislators in one state have already expressed skepticism about the veracity of provider-provided data. To their credit, at least two states are planning supplemental validation studies to further investigate provider-rating-based evaluation procedures.

MINIMIZING SKEPTICISM
ABOUT PROVIDER RATINGS

The most compelling route out of this quandary may have already been suggested by the multidimensional assessment wisdom of many of the program evaluation studies cited earlier. It is now commonplace for evaluators to include in outcome evaluation designs multiple measures assessing different aspects of consumers' adjustment. Perhaps the most straightforward approach, until we know more, is to consider consumer, significant other, and provider ratings as *independent* measures, representing unique perspectives. The ratings by the different sources can then be compared. If there is high agreement this would strengthen the conclusions drawn.

If there are compelling reasons to use providers as the primary sources of outcome data, several strategies may mitigate concerns about possible unintentionally inflated ratings. First, *what* the providers are asked to rate could be limited to consumer behaviors that are observed by the providers in treatment and rehabilitation settings. One example is ratings of consumer progress toward certain treatment goals (see Kuhlman, Sincaban, & Bernstein, 1990, for an example of the use of adapted goal attainment scaling to assess state hospital inpatients' treatment progress). Another example might be including provider ratings of family relationship behavior only if the providers have seen the marital couples, or parents and children, in conjoint interviews or in home visits.

A second strategy, if providers are to rate community functioning, would be to stipulate that the providers have to interview or seek input from other people who do see the consumers regularly outside the treatment setting. Intensive case managers who work with consumers in vivo would be excellent sources of information about consumer behavior. A third strategy might be for mental health agencies to "trade" staff members who would provide ratings but who would be functioning more like independent observers or raters than if they were assessing their own clients. A fourth strategy has to do with the nature of the rating instrument used. To the extent that the various rating points on the scales are described in concrete behavioral terms, the less the ratings are likely to be influenced by extraneous subjective provider factors. An example of such a rating instrument is the HRSD described in Chapter 5. Unfortunately, such behaviorally anchored rating scales are relatively few in number.

At a minimum, however, if provider ratings are to be used as a major source of outcome information, credibility will be enhanced by the inclusion of outcome information from other sources in addition. Recall that it is common in evaluation studies for consumers to improve in some domains of adjustment, not change in others, and occasionally appear to have become worse in some other areas. Thus, it is important to assess multiple dimensions of consumer adjustment, and *from multiple source perspectives.*

When state agencies, funding sources, governing bodies, and/or management are considering outcome evaluation mandates and the use of provider ratings, there are two additional issues to consider. One issue is the aforementioned hassle–irritability factor experienced by clinicians already burdened by extensive paperwork and large caseloads. Resentment can result in haphazard, inconsistent, and unreliable completion of the outcome rating forms with unknown effects on the veracity of the results. The second issue to be considered is the cost of clinicians' time. Although significantly less than other forms of obtaining outcome data, some time is involved and the effects on morale are not inconsequential. An alternative consideration, at possibly no more or only slightly more cost, is the selection of self-administering self-report questionnaires that can be administered by trained and sociable clerical personnel. This can be done successfully with only a slight amount of initial management oversight. Whose time is more expensive, clinicians or clerical staff?

Managers and evaluators need to become creative in developing methods to counteract concerns about vested interests when providers are to be the sources of the outcome data. As indicated earlier, the suspicion of conflicts of interest may be more damaging to the credibility of results than the vested interests themselves. The mental health field needs to continue investigation of the similarity of and differences between different sources of outcome information about the various aspects of consumers' adjustment.

DATA LOSS OR CONSUMER ATTRITION

Regardless of the comparison strategy that is used, the usual intent of the evaluators is that the cohort receiving the service of interest is "like" other clients in the same setting, or perhaps like consumers receiving that kind of service elsewhere. That is, it is hoped that findings can be applied or generalized to consumers other than those being studied. This is the *representativeness* of the cohort issue. It is commonly, and appropriately, assumed that consumers admitted to service during, say, a chosen 6-month period are generally like other consumers admitted during other time periods. This is an appropriate assumption as long as there have been no significant changes in the service, funding, fees, and marketing, and as long as outcome data are obtained from *a large majority* of the consumers in the cohort (and comparison groups if such are part of the study design).

The problem introduced here is that of cohort *attrition*, or data loss, which may possibly result in biased data. Inevitably, some consumers will refuse to participate, and admission or discharge assessments will be missed for others.

The problem is that after the cohort has been reduced by refusals or missed assessments, the remaining members of the cohort are often no longer like consumers in that setting in general. It has now been repeatedly demonstrated that consumers who are cooperative and willing and able to provide outcome data are generally healthier, better adjusted, and have more resources of almost all kinds than consumers from whom it is not possible to obtain complete data for whatever reason (e.g., Epstein, McCrady, Miller, & Steinberg, 1994; Norton, Breitner, Welsh & Wyse, 1994; Speer & Zold, 1971). Such cooperative, self-selected consumers tend to have those demographic, social, and clinical characteristics that are associated with positive response to treatment. Those consumers with the fewest resources and the most difficult problems are often underrepresented in the final analyses.

An example was provided by Speer and Swindle's (1982) study of the 3-month postadmission outcomes among adult outpatients seen at a community mental health center. In this study, consumers completed the Symptom Checklist—90 (SCL-90) at admission, and the follow-up form was sent to them by mail 3 months later with the request to complete the form and return it by mail. Initial inspection suggested that the improvement rates in one 6-month cohort were perceptibly lower than in another cohort. Further examination, however, indicated that the higher cohort-improvement rate was associated with a lower proportion of severely troubled consumers in that cohort providing follow-up data than in the other cohort. Another example is Pekarik's (1992) finding that outpatient consumers who discontinue treatment after only a few sessions have more severe symptoms at admission than do consumers who receive services for a longer period of time.

If attrition or data loss rates are high (e.g., greater than 30–40%), there is a significant possibility that the remainder cohort will have more resources and be more positively responsive to the service than a cohort with less lost follow-up data (i.e., it will be a biased subgroup of all those originally eligible for inclusion in the cohort). The consequence is that this remainder group may produce improvement findings that are atypically higher than would be obtained from a more complete group of the original cohort; improvement rates may be artificially inflated. Conclusions drawn from such a truncated consumer group may suggest greater program effectiveness than is true for all consumers receiving that service.

A word about consumer participation, or data completion, *rates*: different evaluators sometimes compute these rates differently. Keep in mind that evaluators want outcome findings to be based on consumer cohorts that are as representative of all consumers served by the program as possible. One approach is to include all consumers who are stipulated to have received service in the initial consumer cohort pool from which the evaluation cohort is developed (among outpatients this may be consumers who have receved 2–3 or more counseling sessions; among consumers receiving intensive case management services this may be only those who have remained in the program a minimum of 1 month). The participation, or data completion, rate is computed by dividing the number of consumers from whom follow-up information is obtained by the number of consumers in the initial cohort of consumers who received services (i.e., all consumers admitted to service during the time period stipulated to define the cohort). Completion rates based on by-mail requests for follow-up information, with several reminder letters, using this approach are usually in the 40–50% range (e.g., Schainblatt, 1977).

A second approach used by some evaluators is to begin with inviting consumers to participate in the evaluation study, and then computing the participation rate by dividing the number who provide follow-up information by the number who *consent* to participate. Usually about 65% of consumers consent to be followed up. Among these consumers, 70–80% will generally provide follow-up data; however, these consumers will still only constitute 40–50% of all consumers initially eligible for inclusion in the cohort, including those who consent to be followed up and those who do not. In order to avoid confusion, and to obtain a clearer picture of the proportion of all service recipients upon whom the evaluation is based, I favor the first approach. In either case, it is important to compare those who participate in the follow-up assessments with those who do not on an array of pretreatment sociodemographic and clinical variables in order to determine in what ways the participating consumers may not be representative of all clients in the program.

Data loss is inevitable. The issue is a matter of degree and attempting to minimize data loss. When the decision is made that an outcome evaluation study will be done, it is recommended that management and program directors set the objective of obtaining complete admission and second-point assessment data from 90% or more of the cohort. In outpatient programs, making team leaders and program directors responsible for the completion rates at admission can result in initial completion rates of 90% and higher (Speer, 1978). Conclusions drawn from cohorts with attritition rates of 30% or more should be offered with caution.

STRATEGIES FOR DEALING WITH POTENTIAL DATA LOSS AND ATTRITION

In thinking about minimizing attrition, it is helpful to consider that there are at least two phases in outcome evaluation: consumer adjustment during and/or at the end of treatment, and consumer adjustment at some point in time after the termination of treatment or service. The latter is referred to as *follow-up* outcome evaluation and the concern being addressed is the *durability* of the consequences of the mental health service. Here the concern is what are the levels of adjustment and functioning at some interval after cessation of services.

It is a simple truism in outcome evaluation that consumers tend to be more cooperative with assessments while they are receiving services, and notoriously "unavailable" to participation in outcome assessments after they have left treatment. In fact, the participation or completion rates reported above of 40–50% usually involve sizable proportions of consumers who were no longer receiving services (e.g., Schainblatt, 1977; Speer & Swindle, 1982). As a consequence, given strategic planning of assessments, it is often possible to obtain higher participation rates if measures are administered during, towards the end of, or at termination of treatment than if solicited after termination of services.

A general principle is that the more service effectiveness or outcome assessments are made a routine part of agency procedures, whether during or after treatment, the greater is the likelihood that consumers will participate in the assessment process. This is of course a policy matter that may require the support of the governing body, funding sources, and top level management. Thus, education at all levels of the care-providing system is important. The implementation of outcome evaluation is often made complicated because such efforts are treated as special research projects that are not part of routine service delivery management. Completing questionnaires as a routine part of the total service delivery process (including management) is one thing; participation in a research project is something else. This is *not* to say that consumer-informed consent can or should be slighted. Consumers always have the right to say no, just as they have the right to refuse treatment of any kind. This is perhaps a matter of organizational or system attitude conveying concern about the consequences of service for consumers during and after completion of treatment.

A related matter is the potential helpfulness of consumer advocacy groups such as the Alliances for the Mentally Ill at the national, state, and local levels. Service effectiveness and outcomes should be a preeminent concern of such groups. They should also be concerned that low consumer participation rates in outcome evaluation may lead to conclusions that inflate or exaggerate the effectiveness of services. It is hoped that the assertive support of and encouragement of consumers to participate in outcome evaluations would lead to higher participation rates, particularly in follow-up evaluations. It is difficult to improve care systems if we do not know in what areas they are being ineffective.

As indicated above, consumers tend to be more willing to participate in evaluations while they are still receiving service, regardless of whether this is outpatient, inpatient, partial hospitalization, case management, or any of the variety of community support services. The major complication is that consumers often discontinue or drop out of services unilaterally and without letting providers know in advance; that is, they often terminate treatment without the providers knowing it. This is particularly well documented among outpatients, approximately 50% of whom unilaterally and quietly discontinue treatment (Phillips, 1991). This obviously complicates obtaining discharge or termination outcome evaluation assessments from a sizable proportion of consumers.

One strategy for increasing consumer participation rates, is frequent repeated administrations, particularly if brief self-administering questionnaires such as selected scales from the Brief Symptom Inventory, one of Cohen's Perceived Stress Scales, or the General Well-Being scale are used. Among outpatients this might be at admission, after the second and fourth treatment sessions, and less frequently thereafter. This early frequency is recommended because about 50% of outpatients receive four or fewer service contacts (Phillips, 1991). The reasoning here is that if the termination or discharge administration is missed among a sizable proportion of consumers who discontinue treatment unannounced, the chances of having a second administration available are increased. Speer (1994) has reported findings suggesting that "late in service episode" assessments are reasonably good proxies for missed termination assessments. He estimated that use of such end-of-service proxy assessments may underestimate improvement rates by only about 2%. Using this approach, Speer obtained admission and at least one additional assessment for 84% of a cohort of older adult outpatients. Repeated assessments may contribute to consumers' perceptions that the organization cares about how they are doing, and that the assessments are a routine part of the service process.

Turning to follow-up or after termination of service outcome evaluations we are confronted with an enigmatic situation. Here, the usual participation rate, based on all consumers eligible for inclusion in the cohort rather than just those who consent, is generally in the 35–50% range. For example, Lehman, Postrado, Roth, McNary, and Goldman (1994) in their evaluation of case management services for adults with chronic mental illness were able to obtain outcome data from only 40% of the targeted cohort; Peters, Kearns, Murrin, Dolente, and May (1993) were able to get follow-up data from about 55% and 60% of inmates receiving time-limited substance abuse treatment in jail; Lantican and Mayora (1993) had a return rate of only 37% of mailed follow-up questionnaires among female inpatients; and Nicholson (1989) obtained posttreatment mailed returns from parents of 50% of teenage outpatients.

If we are to achieve participation rates in the desired 70–90% range among consumers after they have ceased receiving services, we somehow need to create among them the sense that providing follow-up information is a part of business as usual and that it is in the best interests of consumers in general to participate. Solicitation of the support and encouragement of consumer advocate groups and consumers themselves will probably help with credibility. Use of either paid or volunteer consumers with reasonable social skills as data collectors and interviewers will probably also help. Some evaluators have been able to provide participating consumers with $5–10 payments for participation and found this to increase participation. A basic and necessary strategy is to plan to make multiple follow-up contacts by mail or telephone if participation is not readily forthcoming.

A rarely used prospective strategy is to introduce the follow-up process at the time the consumer is admitted to service or shortly thereafter. Although consumers can always retract or cancel earlier consent agreements, obtaining agreement early on can create the expectation that the organization will be getting in touch with them later on. Some evaluators have asked consumers for the names and addresses of friends or relatives that may know their whereabouts in the event that they should move or leave the state.

Although decision makers may not want to hear this in times of constricting resources, it may be necessary to invest greater financial resources in follow-up outcome evaluations for a while in order to obtain high enough participation that we can have confidence in the results. In our present state of knowledge, it often requires significant time on the part of data collectors just to locate consumers, particularly those who tend to be transient. In an important sense, how consumers are adjusting and functioning 6 months to 2 years after discharge from treatment or service is the bottom line in mental health outcome evaluation. For the foreseeable future administrators may need to accept the expense of discovering the bottom-line results in which one can have confidence. I will return to the subject of consumer attrition in follow-up or durability of treatment effects evaluation in Chapter 7.

TO TEST STATISTICALLY
OR NOT TO TEST STATISTICALLY?

The booby trap introduced here is the adequacy of cohort sizes required to justify statistical tests. Generally this will not be a problem in evaluations where the cohorts are large (defined below). The problem has to do with statistical "power," or the sensitivity of the statistical test to detect statistically significant differences when these differences really exist. From a statistical standpoint, the smaller the cohort sizes the less power or sensitivity the tests have (other things being equal). The problem is that if the cohorts are small, and the statistical test suggests that there is no difference, we cannot determine whether "no difference" really exists or whether "no difference" is an artifact or an extraneous consequence of cohorts that are too small (lack adequate power). Conversely, with small cohorts, if the test suggests a statistically significant difference, there is no problem.

Although this issue is not unique to program evaluation, it may be a greater risk because of the practical problems involved in obtaining outcome data from sizable numbers of consumers. The recent review of published outcome evaluation studies by Speer and Newman (1996) suggests that the problem of small cohort sizes is occasionally a problem even in published reports.

Another way of stating this risk is that cohorts that are too small from a statistical power standpoint are biased against finding statistically significant differences. One risk to drawing a valid conclusion is the situation in which one believes that an innovative service is more effective than the usual service approach. If the cohorts are too small, one may not find a statistically significant difference. Evaluators have thus "shot themselves in the foot" because not enough consumers participated in the evaluation. An example of this situation is Rattenbury and Stones (1989) study of the effectiveness of Reminiscence Group Therapy relative to a current events discussion group and a "no-group" condition among nursing home residents. Only eight consumers participated in each type of group and the no-group situation. Among eight statistical comparisons, only one was found to be significant. Eight participants in each of three groups is markedly too few for a fair statistical test (see below). Was Reminiscence Group Therapy ineffective, or were there simply too few consumers to tell?

A particularly dangerous situation, when cohorts that are too small are involved and no differences are found, is when the evaluator is tempted to conclude that the innovative service is "no worse" than the alternative or usual service. Lack of statistical sensitivity cuts both ways. Reality may be that the innovative service is in fact harmful or less effective than the alternative, but because of the small groups we do not detect the difference. It is important to keep in mind that just as some consumers become worse while receiving services so are some innovative programs less effective than usual services (e.g., Soloman et al's., 1992, study of a residential alternative to usual military treatment of combat veterans with posttraumatic stress disorder).

Two examples of outcome evaluation studies in which the evaluators risked drawing the erroneous conclusion that one service is "as good as" or conversely no worse than another service follow. Hoffman, DiRito, and McGill (1993) studied the effectiveness of a psychoeducational track for thought-disordered consumers in a program for comorbid mentally ill and substance-abusing adults. They found no differences on a number of variables, and concluded that the cognitively impaired consumers did as well with the psychoeducational program as did the other consumers who received the standard treatment. However, there were only 12 consumers in one group and 18 in the other. Hiday and Scheid-Cook (1989) compared three groups of persistently and severely mentally ill adults: those involuntarily committed to outpatient treatment, those committed to a hospital, and those released from commitment. Six months later there were no differences among the groups on the vast majority of outcome measures studied. However, there were only 38, 11, and 50 consumers in the three groups; about half the number needed for a fair test.

Fortunately there are some guidelines for determining the desirable number of consumers per group for fair statistical tests (i.e., for tests that will not suggest misleading conclusions). Cohen (1992) has suggested for moderate-sized group differences, consensually accepted reasonable statistical sensitivity (power = .80) and p = .05 or less, that 65 consumers per group are needed for comparing two groups. For comparing three groups, 50 consumers per group will result in an appropriately sensitive and fair test, and so on. If only one group of consumers is being studied over time (i.e., repeatedly assessed on several occasions), Kraemer and Thiemann's (1987) methodology suggest that a group of 36 will produce adequate test sensitivity for a medium-sized service effect.

The difference in desirable group sizes for multiple group comparisons and for testing change in a single group appears counterintuitive. The advantage for a single group that is repeatedly assessed over time is a result of the test having a built-in control for individual differences among the consumers at the first assessment. As a result, fewer consumers are needed to detect a significant change than if groups of different consumers are being compared. The moral here is that fewer participants are needed, if they are assessed on two or more occasions, than if two groups are assessed only once, say at discharge, and compared.

Where does this leave the small-scale service program that may be intensively treating only a few consumers over an extended period of time and wants to evaluate its outcomes? What about the principle that "some outcome data are better than no outcome data"? The principle still holds. The reader should be reminded that statistical tests are simply tools to help the evaluator make reasonable judgments and draw justifiable conclusions. In this situation, the tools may be inappropriate to the task. However, it is helpful to summarize the data in some way that lends itself to making inferences about how consumers in the program are doing.

There are several approaches. One approach, when cohorts are too small for testing, is to simply compute and report percentages of consumers in various categories of outcomes. For example, Lerner, Sigal, Bacalu, and Gelkopf (1992) in a study of 17 opioid- dependent adults in short-term and 17 in long-term psychotherapy did not statistically test their data. Instead, they simply reported the percentages of each group who were abstinent during treatment, dropped out of therapy, and reentered treatment. Some differences, such as the 63% in short-term versus 22% in long-term who reentered therapy, have considerable face validity. Similarly, Asay and Dimperio (1991) simply reported the percentages of parents of former child psychiatry inpatients who described the young person as "much" or "greatly" improved at 1 year follow-up (68%). Bath, Richey, and Haapala (1992) simply reported the percentage of children, at risk for removal from their own homes, who were still in their own homes 1 year after admission to an intensive community family-oriented treatment program (83%).

Another nontest approach is to plot consumer average scores over time on graphs. In a study of 20 persistently and severely mentally ill older adults in a supported housing program, O'Sullivan and Speer (1995) graphed the average depression, physical symptoms and stress scores of those consumers in independent apartments and those in adult foster homes. The consumers had been assessed on four occasions over a 2-year period. The two groups differed noticeably on most of the outcome variables. Furthermore, neither group of consumers changed noticeably during the 2-year period.

If justifiable criteria for "improvement" or significant change can be agreed upon, data can be reported in terms of percentages of consumers improved, unchanged, and deteriorated. Using the number of referral problems subsequently rated as less severe by providers, Speer et al. (1996) reported that 55% of nursing home residents were much improved and 8% worse following mental health intervention. Using a somewhat more cumbersome statistical process for testing individual consumer change (see Chapter 3), Speer (1994) found that 51% of older adult mental health outpatients had improved, whereas 5% became worse following outpatient treatment.

A potential fringe benefit of not using statistical tests to evaluate outcome information is that we are often forced to develop reporting methods that may be intrinsically more comprehensible to decision makers than are traditional scientific methods. However, without the guidance of statistical tests, greater professional judgment and responsibility is required of the evaulator in interpreting the data and drawing conclusions. A moderately conservative (i.e., humble) approach is recommended.

"HELLO" AND "GOOD-BYE" EFFECTS

This potential source of bias and risk for drawing misleading conclusions is based on a clinical observation by the author rather than being based on data. I was piloting an outcome monitoring system in a psychiatric inpatient unit in a community mental health center using the SCL-90. I was also doing some clinical work with a few of the consumers on the unit. The consumers were asked to complete the symptom checklist soon after admission and again just prior to being discharged. The inpatient unit accepted only voluntary clients and was an unlocked unit. The admission and discharge data from 30–40 consumers was startling. As a group they reported *extreme*, almost off-the-scale symptomatology at admission and generally normal level symptomatology at discharge (the average length of stay was about 30 days). The data suggested that the inpatient unit was having amazing "cure" rates.

Observation and talking with some of the consumers suggested another interpretation of the findings. Most of the consumers were in severe crises and in very stressful and conflictual situations at admission. Most were in desperate need of relief. Thus, it appeared that consumers tended to exaggerate their symptoms to "make sure" they were admitted and received care. After a few weeks of treatment, and peace, they became motivated to return to the community. Thus, they appeared to underreport their symptoms prior to discharge to "make sure" they could leave without discomforting hassles. The "hello" effect is the tendency to exaggerate problems as a possible cry for help and to emphasize the need for help. The "good-bye" effect is the tendency to minimize problems to justify termination of services. Putting these two reporting tendencies together can result in a program appearing almost unbelievably effective.

In the scientific literature, these potential biases are usually considered examples of *situational demand biases*. These are biases that are fostered by the situations and circumstances in which consumers find themselves, as they perceive and interpret them, which lead them to alter the way they respond to assessment questions or items. Among inpatient consumers, a fairer assessment of their posttreatment adjustment is at some time after they have left the inpatient unit and returned to the community. Sperry, Brill, Howard, and Grissom (1996) suggest 1-month post discharge.

Another example of a "demanding" situation that may lead to misleading responses is when the service provider interviews the consumer about his or her satisfaction with the services he or she has received. It is difficult to tell your counselor or helper, to his or her face, that you think he or she has done less than wonderful work with you; the situation almost demands favorable responses.

It is important for evaluators to keep these situational dynamics in mind when designing evaluations and in interpreting the findings. Because we are not attempting to be highly scientific about our evaluations, there is greater opportunity for unintended distortions to creep into the data collection and interpretation processes. Some degree of skepticism about our evaluation work may alleviate some embarrassment during reporting to policy and decision makers.

DO EMOTIONS AND BEHAVIOR CHANGE AT THE SAME RATE?

The answer to this question is, apparently not. In 1975, Ellsworth first reported the observation that consumers in the VA system appeared to start "feeling better" well in advance of their beginning to display behavioral changes. I had the same experience while pilot testing a self-report measure of emotions and various behaviors among outpatient adults seen at a community mental health center. These consumers reported significant improvements in mood and comfort often after only two or three therapy sessions. Significant changes in interpersonal behavior, communication, and role behaviors generally did not start appearing until significantly later. More recently, Howard, Lueger, Maling and Martinovich (1993) reported similar findings in a study of over 450 adult mental health outpatients. They found that improvements in consumers' subjective well-being preceded significant symptomatic improvement, which in turn preceded significant changes in consumers' lifestyles, habits, and personality characteristics.

These findings may shed light on the propensity of adult outpatients to discontinue treatment after only a few therapy sessions. Some consumers who start feeling better discontinue treatment because it was their distress that motivated them to request service, and when the distress improves they see no reason to continue treatment.

The trap, or risk for drawing misleading conclusions, here is that if one assesses either emotional or behaviorial variables alone one may arrive at an inaccurate picture of consumers' change. If one measures emotions alone, one might conclude that consumers improve quite rapidly; if one assesses only behavioral characteristics, we might conclude that change is a long-term process. This again supports the recommendation that ideally we should be assessing multiple aspects of consumers' adjustment. This situation also suggests that a sophisticated perspective on the service program's goal is required vis-à-vis selection of program-appropriate measures. Measures appropriate for outcome assessment in a crisis service may not be appropriate for a treatment program with longer term objectives.

In summary, several evaluation issues that may confound our data collection and reporting of outcome findings have been discussed. Specifically, the complications arising from use of provider ratings, the inability to enlist the cooperation of a relatively high proportion of consumers in the study cohort, statistical tests when groups are too small, situations that "demand" certain responses from consumers, and the fact that affect and behavior change at different rates were reviewed. None of these risks of misleading results are prohibitive. However, the evaluator must be aware of these potential biases and must qualify conclusions accordingly when they are likely to have influenced the data.

REFERENCES

Asay, T. P., & Dimperio, T. L. (1991). Outcome of children treated in psychiatric hospitals. In S. M. Mirin, J. T. Gossett & M. C. Grob (Eds.), *Psychiatric treatment: Advances in outcome research* (pp. 21–30). Washington, DC: American Psychiatric Press.

Bath, H. I., Richey, C. A., & Haapala, D. A. (1992). Child age and outcome correlates in intensive family preservation services. *Children and Youth Services Review, 14,* 389–406.

Becker, M., Diamond, R., & Sainfort, F. (1993). A new patient focused index for measuring quality of life in persons with severe and persistent mental illness. *Quality of Life Research, 2,* 239–251.

Cohen, J. (1992). A power primer. *Psychological Bulletin, 112,* 155–159.

Ellsworth, R. B. (1975). Consumer feedback in measuring the effectiveness of mental health programs. In M. Guttentay & E. L. Struenning (Eds.), *Handbook of evaluation research* (Vol. 2, pp. 239–274). Beverlyh Hills: Sage.

Epstein, E. E., McCrady, B. S., Miller, K. J., & Steinberg, M. (1994). Attrition from conjoint alcoholisme treatment: Do dropouts differ from completers? *Journal of Substance Abuse, 6,* 249–265.

Hiday, V. A., & Scheid-Cook, T. L. (1989). A follow-up of chronic patients committed to outpatient treatment. *Hospital and Community Psychiatry, 40,* 52–59.

Hoffman, G. W., DiRito, D. C., & McGill, E. C. (1993). Three-month follow-up of 28 Dual diagnosis inpatients. *American Journal of Drug and Alcohol Abuse, 19,* 79–88.

Howard, K. I., Lueger, R. J., Maling, M. S., & Martinovich, Z. (1993). A phase model of psychotherapy outcome: Causal mediation of change. *Journal of Consulting and Clinical Psychology, 61,* 678–685.

Kraemer, H. C., & Thiemann, S. (1987). *How many subjects?* Newbury Park, CA: Sage.

Kuhlman, T. L., Sincaban, V. A., & Bernstein, M. J. (1990). Team use of the global assessment scale for inpatient planning and evaluation. *Hospital and Community Psychiatry, 41,* 416–419.

Lambert, M. J., Hatch, D. R., Kingston, M. D., & Edwards, B. C. (1986). Zung, Beck, and Hamilton rating scales as measures of treatment outcome: A meta-analytic comparison. *Journal of Consulting and Clinical Psychology, 54,* 54–59.

Lambert, M. J., & Hill, C. E. (1994). Assessing psychotherapy outcomes and process. In A. E. Bergin & S. L. Garfield (Eds.), *Handbook of psychotherapy and behavior change* (pp. 72–113). New York: John Wiley.

Lantican, L. S. M., & Mayorga, J. (1993). Effectiveness of a women's mental health treatment program: A pilot study. *Issues in Mental Health Nursing, 14,* 31–49.

Lehman, A. E., Postrado, L. T., Roth, D., McNary, S. W., & Goldman, H. H. (1994). Continuity of care and client outcomes in the Robert Wood Johnson Foundation program on chronic mental illness. *Milbank Quearterly, 72,* 105–122.

Lerner, A., Sigal, M., Bacalu, A., & Gelkopf, M. (1992). Short term versus long term psychotherapy in opioid dependence: A pilot study. *International Journal of Psychiatry and Related Sciences, 29,* 114–119.

Massey, O. T., & Wu, L. (1994). Three critical views of functioning: Comparisons of assessments made by individuals with mental illness, their case managers, and family members. *Evaluation and Program Planning, 17,* 1–7.

Nicholson, S. (1989). Outcome evaluation of therapeutic effectiveness. *The Australian and New Zealand Journal of Family Therapy, 10,* 77–83.

Norton, M. C., Breitner, J. C. S., Welsh, K. A., & Wyse, B. W. (1994). Characteristics of nonresponders in a community survey of the elderly. *Journal of the American Geriatrics Society, 42,* 1252–1256.

O'Sullivan, M., & Speer, D. C. (1995). *The supported housing program, Broward County Elderly Services, Ft. Lauderdale, FL: Evaluation final report.* Tampa, FL: Florida Mental Health Institute.

Pekarik, G. (1992). Posttreatment adjustment of clients who drop out early vs. late in treatment. *Journal of Clinical Psychology, 48,* 379–387.

Peters, R. A., Kerns, W. D., Murrin, M. R., Dolente, A. S., & May, R. L. (1993). Examining the effectiveness of in-jail substance abuse treatment. *Journal of Offender Rehabilitation, 19,* 1–39.

Phillips, E. L. (1991). George Washington University international data on psychotherapy delivery systems: Modeling new approaches to the study of therapy. (In L. E. Beutler & M. Crago (Eds.), *Psychotherapy research: An international review of programmatic studies* (pp. 263–273). Washington, DC: American Psychological Association.

Rattenbury, C., & Stones, M. J. (1989). A controlled evaluation of reminiscence and current topics discussion groups in nursing homes. *The Gerontologist, 29,* 768–771.

Schainblatt, A. H. (1977). *Monitoring the outcomes of state mental health treatment programs: Some initital suggestions.* Washington, DC: The Urban Institute.

Solomon, Z., Shalev, A., Spiro, S. E., Dolev, A., Bleich, A., Waysman, M., & Cooper, S. (1992). Negative psychometric outcomes: Self-report measures and a follow-up telephone survey. *Journal of Traumatic Stress, 5,* 225–246.

Speer, D. C. (1978, August-September). *Effects of executive policy on client consent and participation rates, and exemplifying outcome results.* Paper presented at the 86th Annual Convention of the American Psychological Association, Toronto, Canada.

Speer, D. C. (1994). Can treatment research inform decision makers? Nonexperimental method issues and examples among older outpatients. *Journal of Consulting and Clinical Psychology, 62,* 560–568.

Speer, D. C., & Newman, F. L. (1996). Mental health services outcome evaluation. *Clinical Psychology: Science and Practice, 3,* 105–129.

Speer, D. C., O'Sullivan, M. J., & Lester, W. A. (1996). Impact of mental health services in nursing homes: The clinicians' perspective. *Journal of Clinical Geropsychology, 2,* 83–92.

Speer, D. C., & Swindle, R. (1982). The "monitoring model" and the mortality X treatment interaction threat to validity in mental health outcome evaluation. *American Journal of Community Psychology, 10,* 541–552.

Speer, D. C., & Zold, A. C. (1971). An example of self-selection bias in follow-up research. *Journal of Clinical Psychology, 27,* 64–68.

Sperry, L., Brill, P. L., Howard, K. I., & Grissom, G. R. (1996). *Treatment outcomes in psychotherapy and psychiatricinterventions.* New York: Brunner/Mazel.

CHAPTER 7

Practical Implementation
Issues and Suggestions

Thus far I have discussed some of the practical needs for outcome evaluation, a less scientific but hopefully more practical conceptual framework for outcome evaluation, comparisions that facilitate the interpretation and communication of outcome information, a variety of outcome measures, and some pitfalls that may lead to misleading conclusions. In this chapter, an attempt is made to pull these various issues together in the form of an overview of beginning implementation issues, some examples of outcome evaluation approaches, and some practical suggestions for implementation.

In planning an evaluation, a number of issues need to be considered and decided. These issues include at least (a) for whom the evaluation is being conducted, (b) the nature of the clientele being served, (c) whether an ongoing or a new (or changed) program is to be evaluated, and (d) whether the immediate impact or the durability of the effects of the service is being evaluated. Decisions about these issues will in turn focus decision-making processes about *what* is to be measured and the *comparisons* to be used in interpreting the outcome information. Finally, there are the practical matters of actual data collection.

FOR WHOM?

The planning of any evaluation should begin with serious consideration of the impetus for the evaluation. It is perhaps stating the obvious, but the likelihood that outcome information will be taken seriously and used by decision makers will largely be a function of the degree to which the evaluation addresses the particular informational interests and needs of the decision makers. At the simplest level is whether the evaluation is being mandated, requested, or recommended by an entity external to the provider organization, or whether it is being initiated by the provider organization itself. External entities may be legislative bodies, major funding sources, managed care organizations, regulatory or licensing bodies, or accrediting organizations. Unfortunately, at the time of this writing, the needs for specific kinds of outcome information by particular funding and regulatory organizations are not clear and are likely to change in the short run.

Different instigating entities will likely have different outcome information interests and needs. They will also quite likely operate from different assumption and value frameworks. These different needs and belief systems will have implications for the planning and implementation of the outcome evaluation. For example, legislators may be primarily interested in whether or not consumers are employed and self-supporting at the end of the treatment episode, whereas accrediting agencies might be more interested in consumers' social support systems or coping resources. Funding sources, on the other hand, might want to know about the extent of distress and symptom reduction, and/or the prevalence of rehospitalization and lengths of stay.

As mentioned earlier, some elected officials are skeptical about outcome data that originate with service providers, such as rating scales completed by the clinicians. This needs to be determined through conversations with representative officials, or their staff members. The pros and cons, sources of misleading information, and costs of various approaches should be discussed, and a consensus reached on the approach to be implemented. If skepticism is minimal and trust high, provider ratings are an economical way to go. If skepticism exists, self-report questionnaires are an option, perhaps at the cost of a part-time clerical person in each agency. If the decision makers prefer completely independent data sources, independent interviewers are a possibility but at a relatively high cost. The financial feasibility of such a strategy might be enhanced by obtaining data from a sample of provider agencies rather than all agencies in a city, district, or state system, or from samples of consumers rather than entire cohorts.

An important matter to be clarified with external evaluation instigators is the relative importance to them of information about where consumers stand on a measure in relation to the general population or nonconsumers. Part of this discussion must include the unfortunate fact that measures of functioning and role performance often do not have norms available. However, some questions about functioning have such high face validity that the matter of norms is obviated (e.g., are you employed, have you been homeless during the past month?).

On the other hand, some third-party payer and managed care organizations appear satisfied with provider-based diagnoses, treatment plans, and reports of progress toward treatment goals. On the belief that payers may want different kinds of outcome information at some time in the future, some provider agencies are preempting the process by beginning to explore additional or alternative methods for evaluating the outcomes of their services (e.g., Sperry, Brill, Howard, & Grissom, 1996). The long-term fruitfulness of such an effort may be enhanced by soliciting the input of prominent payers or managed care organizations. Given the current atmosphere of urgency, flux, and uncertainty, it is possible that some third-party payers and funding sources may simply accept the outcome evaluation methods in use by service providers rather than thinking through the criteria for effective services from their own standpoint. The ideal situation is a collaborative relationship between funding or policy organizations and provider organizations in which the outcome methodology is developed that addresses the needs of the former.

If the impetus for the outcome evaluation is the provider organization itself, there may be greater latitude in decisions about methods. However, management and staff would be well advised to seriously consider what they want to know and why they want to know it. For example, even though external sources of revenue do not appear interested in measures of psychopathology, an instrument such as the Brief Psychiatric Rating Scales (BPRS; Overall & Gorham, 1962) may be of greater practical interest to the clinical staff and the internal quality assurance processes than other kinds of measures. If the BPRS is selected by clinical staff and program directors to investigate how different types of consumers respond to individual, group, or family therapy, vested interest dynamics may be less of an issue than under other circumstances. That is, "looking good" to self or others may not be relevant to the purposes of the evaluation.

In any event, the provider organization will be well served by investing some time in thinking through why they are going to do what they are going to do and how the results are likely to be used. A well-thought-out rationale and plan can be persuasive in negotiations with external and funding entities.

THE NATURE OF THE CLIENTELE

It is tempting to talk in terms of traditional types of mental health services such as outpatient, inpatient, and halfway house programs. However, with the current emphasis on providing the least restrictive and least costly kinds of care that address consumers' needs, the trend is to talk in terms of consumers in crisis, those who can benefit from ambulatory care, assessment of functional impairment and resources, and the persistence or recurrence of consumer problems. Obviously, these various dimensions represent continua with consumers distributing themselves along three or four dimensions simultaneously. In the next section, we will discuss examples of outcome evaluation approaches for three groups of consumers who vary in degree of distress, resources, and functioning.

I am developing some doubts about the utility, and perhaps the validity, of the traditional "acute-chronic" distinction. There is general consensus that some conditions, such as Schizophrenia and Bipolar Disorder, tend to be life-long and thus chronic. The intransigency of various personality disorders to treatment suggest that they tend to be of long-term duration. Evidence is slowly accumulating that many people who experience severe depression and anxiety are prone to relapse or multiple episodes. We need to learn a lot more about the lifetime courses of personality disorders, depression and anxiety, and about the comorbidity of these conditions. This aspect of the medical model may prove to be artificial when applied to mental health problems. As we learn more about the longitudinal courses of varying conditions and their comorbidity, and the incidence of recurring episodes, the current emphasis on palliative and short-term interventions may prove to be cost inefficient from a lifetime cost standpoint. Let us turn now to some sample outcome evaluation approaches.

CONSUMERS WITH HIGH DISTRESS, HIGH RESOURCES, AND RELATIVELY HIGH FUNCTIONING

Here we are interested in evaluating the effectiveness of mental health services for people with moderate to high distress, and moderate to high economic, health, and social resources. Experience in traditional outpatient mental health service settings indicates that the vast majority of consumers request services because of depression, anxiety, and/or family problems. Although their distress may be interfering with the efficiency of their functioning, at lower levels of distress they are generally moderate to high functioning in role performances (e.g., at home, work, and in social relationships).

If the services are being provided in a psychiatric or medical setting, a minimum protocol might consist of the Depression and Anxiety scales of the Brief Symptom Inventory (BSI, Derogatis & Spencer, 1982) and Cohen and Williamson's (1988) Perceived Stress Scale (PSS), for example. These could be supplemented with monthly queries about days of work missed and perhaps health status information. The questionnaires can be easily administered by an intake or clerical person and will take the consumer about 3 minutes to complete.

They could then be readministered by a receptionist at the end of the second, fourth, and as many sessions as planned.

In a nonmedical setting such as a family services association agency, Dupuy's (1977) General Well-Being (GWB) scale, and Procidano and Heller's (1983) Perceived Support from Friends and Family scales might constitute a minimum battery. If the agency emphasizes marital and family therapy, the Expressiveness and Conflict scales from Moos and Moos's (1981) Family Environment Scales (FES) might be considered. These are all self-administering scales and will take consumers about 10–15 minutes to complete. All, except the social support scales, have nonconsumer norms so staff could be provided with monthly summaries. A final or interim report relative to the nonpatient averages and cutoff scores suggesting severe problems also could be provided for governing bodies or external funding sources.

CONSUMERS WITH MODERATE DISTRESS, MARGINAL RESOURCES, AND MARGINAL FUNCTIONING

Such persons may not be experiencing marked anxiety or depression at admission, but may be experiencing a crisis of feeling overwhelmed and hopeless. They may report moderate continual malaise, insecurity, and lack of self-confidence. They may have only a high school education, have difficulty maintaining employment, have limited income because of seasonal or episodic employment, and may have limited interpersonal skills. Here a minimum outcome evaluation battery might include Cohen and Williamson's (1988) PSS and Procidano and Heller's (1983) Perceived Support from Friends and Family Scales. If these consumers are receiving some form of intensive service such as day treatment, consideration might be given to inclusion of selected scales from Riggio's (1986) Social Skills Inventory.

To monitor role functioning, the Living Situation and the Work items from Lehman's et al. (no date) Brief form of the Quality of Life Inventory might be included in the basic battery. Although these items are straightforward with high face validity, the staff persons completing them should spend some time reviewing the manual and conjointly rating a few clients so that the raters are asking the questions and rating the responses in the same manner.

Note that of the measures suggested as examples here, only the PSS has nonconsumer norms. Although for outcome evaluation purposes it is not necessary that all measures have norms, it is strongly recommended that at least one measure with norms be included in the assessment package. Again, this will permit evaluating the cohort's status relative to nonconsumers prior to and following receipt of services.

CONSUMERS WITH MODERATE
TO HIGH DISTRESS, FEW RESOURCES,
AND LOW FUNCTIONING

With these consumers, the array of outcome measures should probably vary according to the types of services they are receiving and which are to be evaluated. For example, if such consumers are regularly hospitalized or served in short-term residential programs for crisis management and medication stabilization, the Depression, Anxiety, Paranoid Ideation, and the Psychoticism scales from the Hopkins Symptom Checklist-90 (Smith, 1996) would be appropriate self-report measures. The BPRS (Overall & Gorham, 1962) might also be considered depending on the orientation of the facility's governing body, management, and the clinical staff. If the second assessment is to occur at discharge, the BPRS scales will be less influenced by the "hello–good-bye" dynamic than self-report measures. If the second assessment is to occur at some point, say 2–3 months after discharge, the self-report symptom measures may be a useful means of assessing posttreatment status. Having nonconsumer norms, these symptom measures will also allow evaluation of the status of the consumers and the cohort relative to members of the general public.

If the services to be evaluated include some form of supervised living arrangement and/or intensive case management, measures of general well-being and stress would be appropriate indicators of consumer distress. For residential programs, completion of the household maintenance, employment/income, and outside social activity scale of the Personal Adjustment and Role Skill scales (PARS, Ellsworth, 1975) by supervisory or monitoring staff would assess some aspects of role performance. For consumers receiving case management, the scales of the Missouri Levels of Care instrument (Kramer, Massey, & Pokorny, 1990) completed by the case manager would be appropriate measures of role functioning in the community. Recall that case managers were found to be conservative raters of some aspects of consumer functioning, and therefore may not appear as subject to conflict-of-interest influences as provider ratings in other circumstances.

COMPARISON AND
INTERPRETATION STRATEGIES

The above comments have provided examples of *what* kinds of outcome variables might be assessed in service programs for consumers who have varying social and economic resources, and varying levels role functioning. What about *comparison* strategies for the interpretation of data? The good news is that measures and comparison strategies are, for the most part, independent of one another. That is, the above examples of outcome measures, and most other measures, can be used with almost any of the comparison strategies described earlier: the single-cohort pre–posttreatment strategy, the nonequivalent comparison group approaches, or the experimental random assignment design. The simplist approach would be the administration of the measures at admission and again, at least once, during or toward the end of service for a single cohort of consumers. This would permit a graphic or statistical comparison of the individual or group average scores at admission with those at a later point, thus permitting consideration of change.

If measures with nonconsumer norms are selected, such as many of the measures of distress and symptoms, the evaluators automatically have the opportunity for a nonequivalent group comparison. That is, individual consumer or group average scores at admission and discharge can be compared with the normative group average and with the cutoff scores, suggesting serious levels of problems. For example, working with individual consumer scores, a tabulation of those on the "serious problem" side of the cutoff score at admission and discharge will give the proportion of consumers with probable significant problems before and at the conclusion of treatment.

The exemplified measures would also lend themselves to other kinds of nonequivalent comparison group investigations. If the effects of a program change are to be studied, the measures could be administered to consumers admitted during the last 3 months prior to implementation of the program change. Their admission and discharge data could then be compared to those of consumers admitted during the first 3 months after the program change.

Similarly, these measures could be used in a randomized experimental study of the effects of a supplemental time-limited structured group stress management course for consumers receiving individual counseling, for example. All consumers receiving individual counseling would be eligible to participate, but only a randomly selected proportion would be offered the stress management class in addition to the individual counseling, whereas the others would continue receiving only their individual counseling.

One trap that evaluation planners need to be aware of is when assessments are made only at discharge in a single-cohort study. Ordinarily, comparisons that incorporate both admission and discharge assessments will be stronger and provide more information than those involving just discharge assessments. If feasibility or economic circumstances permit only discharge assessments, some comparisons with other groups or with norms may be possible. The trap in the single-cohort, posttreatment-assessment-only situation occurs when data from other comparison groups are not available and the measures used do not have nonconsumer norms available; there is no readily available reference point to assist in the interpretation of the discharge only data. If the outcome measure or information has high face validity, the evaluation may still be worth doing in spite of the absence of formal comparison information. This situation indicates why it is important to think through how the outcome data will be interpreted during the planning phase.

NEW, CHANGED, OR ONGOING PROGRAMS?

An important initial issue, with implications for the comparison strategy selected for the evaluation, is whether the outcome evaluation is to focus on an unmodified ongoing program, a new program to be implemented, or involves significant changes in a service program. Related matters are whether or not program changes are to be implemented on a small scale, and whether or not the new or changed program is to be operated simultaneously or parallel with the former service.

If the focus of the outcome evaluation is an unmodified, ongoing program, decision making will primarily involve selection of outcome measures with simultaneous attention being given to the comparisons to be made in drawing effectiveness inferences from the data. As indicated earlier, the least complicated comparison involves examination of differences and changes between outcome measure information obtained at admission and that obtained later and/or toward the end of service. If interest is only in a relatively brief snapshot of the service's outcomes, the cohort may be defined as those consumers admitted during a 3–4-month period. Here an important consideration is whether or not the admission-second point data is to be statistically tested. If "yes," the cohort should be so defined as to assure that admission and later point information will be obtained from a minimum of 35 to 40 consumers.

If management and staff interests are in longer term examination of the stability of the characteristics of the consumers entering the service program and of the effects of the service over a longer period, the strategy might be to study the characteristics and changes within and between 6-month admission cohorts over a 2-year period. The logistics would be the same as above except that the characteristics and changes among consumers admitted during the first 6 months could be compared with those of consumers admitted during the next 6 months, or with those admitted a year later. Consumers admitted during each 6-month period would be defined as a separate cohort and the different cohorts could be compared. Although interest is in an unmodified program, we have slipped into a perhaps more informative nonequivalent comparison group strategy. This perspective might have particularly important policy implications if there has been, for example, a significant change in how the service program is funded, implementation of managed care controls, or changes in the fee structure. Such an ongoing outcome-monitoring approach might also be informative for policy makers if there are probable funding, managed care, or fee structure changes among other mental health service providers in the community. Capitation and prepayment funding arrangements, for example, create pressures particularly among proprietary providers to refer or shift high service-using and more troubled consumers to publicly funded providers.

Of course, the information provided by pre- and postservice evaluation of an ongoing program could be enhanced if at least one measure with public norms is included in the assessment battery. Another approach would be to seek out data from other groups of consumers or people with whom the particular measure has been used (e.g., O'Sullivan and Speer's, 1995, comparison of supported housing consumers with Parkinson's disease patients and caregivers).

With respect to changed or new service programs, one option of course is to simply assess at admission and at later intervals the first 40 or so consumers admitted after the change has been implemented. This would permit the single-cohort pre–postservice comparison evaluation. However, with planning, outcome information could also be obtained from the last 65–70 consumers admitted to the prior program before the implementation of the change. Comparison of the outcome data from these consumers with those of the first 65–70 admitted after ther program change would permit a relatively strong test of the effects of the program change. Note that a larger number of consumers is required in each group for statistical testing than for a single cohort for pre-posttesting only because two *different* groups of individuals are being compared, rather than just change within a single group of the same individuals. This nonequivalent comparison strategy would allow comparisons of two groups of consumers seen at the same agency who presumably would be similiar in demographic and clinical characteristics. The comparison would permit inferences about how consumers fare after receiving the modified service relative to consumers served by the prior service program.

If the modified or new program is to be implemented on a small scale or pilot basis, *and* if the previous service program is to be temporarily continued in parallel to the new program, management and the evaluator have the opportunity to conduct an outcome evaluation that will permit relatively definitive inferences about the impact of the modified program. For example, suppose two or three clinical staff members have received training in a new form of structured and time-limited marital group therapy. Suppose they have convinced management that this new group approach is likely to be more cost-effective than traditional marital counseling. If the number of couples seeking marital help is greater than the number that can be absorbed in the new group program, the ideal circumstances exist for a true experimental evaluation of the new service. After obtaining the appropriate informed consent, the couples agreeing to participate can then simply be randomly assigned to either the new group treatment program or to the preexisting and ongoing marital counseling program.

The randomization process assures (theoretically) that couples in the two samples will be generally equivalent on treatment- pertinent variables and that the two groups will differ only on the treatment they receive. Outcome data from the two groups will provide strong evidence about the efficacy, or absence thereof, of the new group treatment. The Peters, Kearns, Murrin, Dolente, and May (1993) experimental evaluation of a structured group treatment for substance abusers in jail is a good example of capitalizing on demand for service exceeding available resources to conduct a powerful evaluation of a mental health service program.

IMMEDIATE IMPACT OR DURABILITY OF TREATMENT-EFFECT EVALUATIONS

Given the paucity of outcome and effectiveness information from community-based mental health services, documentation of the immediate effects of different kinds of services for consumers with different kinds and constellations of difficulties is important. Although the abundant evidence from laboratory research on psychosocial interventions suggests that community-based services also likely have positive immediate effects for most consumers, greater documentation is necessary. Vast public and private resources are being invested in broad spectrum mental health services. The fiduciary responsibilities of legislatures, funders, and policy makers require evidence.

Obviously, the first step is to demonstrate that services have immediate effects either producing significant positive change or, at a minimum, preventing deterioration or decline in adjustment. A phenomenon called "delayed effects" has been identified from time to time. This is the situation in which consumers do not appear to have changed significantly at the end of service, but demonstrate significant improvements at some later time when follow-up information is obtained. This is the exception rather than the rule, however. If on the average, or for the majority of consumers, we cannot show positive effects during or at the end of treatment, it would be difficult to justify the resources needed to investigate more long-term treatment effects.

As indicated earlier, it is relatively easier to conduct outcome evaluations, with the needed high consumer-participation rates while consumers are receiving services or at the end of services. In fact, all of the examples provided in this chapter were predicated on the assumption that the purpose of the evaluations was to demonstrate immediate treatment impact.

It is *imperative* that the focus of the outcome evaluation, whether on immediate or long-term effects, be carefully considered, explicitly decided, and clearly articulated prior to implementation of the evaluation. A service provider organization considering implementation of immediate-effects outcome evaluation for the first time may experience the process as onerous and difficult. However, with planning, good communication, and training, the evaluation can be implemented relatively easily and inexpensively, perhaps only at the cost of some clerical and management time, and with minimal provider staff time, depending on the purpose for which the evaluation is being done. The process may largely involve the planning of the logistics and designating and training the least expensive staff for data collection and collation.

When turning to the consideration of outcome evaluation of the long-term effects of treatment, or follow-up evaluation after consumers have terminated service, evaluators are confronted with a much more difficult and expensive task. The reason that so little is known about the longer term adjustment of consumers is that longitudinal research and evaluation is fraught with methodological and, occasionally, ethical problems. These solutions may be time-consuming and costly. Injudicious launching of follow-up evaluations has resulted in outcome data that are so incomplete, confounded, or biased that they are difficult if not impossible to interpret (Speer & Newman, 1996).

This is a dilemma of major proportions. Information about the durability of the immediate positive effects of mental health services is needed on the one hand, both to justify the expenditure of vast resources and to provide the information necessary for corrective service management and design. On the other hand, methodological problems and costs are great. For example, the average costs per successfully followed-up consumers have varied from $26 to $650 per consumer (Ribisl et al., 1996). The biggest and most damaging problem is cohort attrition or loss of consumers from the targeted cohort. An excellent recent review and analysis of the attrition problem in longitudinal and follow-up evaluations by Ribisl and his colleagues (1996) has again documented the distortions and biases introduced by failure to obtain follow-up information from 70% or more of the designated cohort. High attrition rates may seriously limit generalization of findings to all the consumers in whom we are primarily interested and put us at risk of drawing misleading conclusions. The most common causes of attrition are inability to find or locate consumers, consumer refusal to participate, and death or disability of the consumer.

The attrition problem is not insoluble. Ribisl et al. (1996) report follow-up studies in which completion rates have ranged above 80% and in a few cases upwards of 90%. These completion rates have been the result of tenacious tracking and considerable persistence on the part of the evaluation staff.

The primary moral here is that the decision to initiate a follow-up evaluation should not be made lightly. In order to obtain information from a sufficient proportion of consumers to provide usable information requires a lot of time, energy, and resources. Management should carefully consider such an initiative and perhaps discuss the need for the evaluation and the costs with funding sources. If supplemental financial resources are not available, the feasibility of such an evaluation may be in question.

Based on their extensive review of the literature, Ribisl and his colleagues (1996) offered a number of broad recommendations to facilitate high consumer-participation rates. Examination of this paper prior to deciding whether or not to conduct a follow-up evaluation is strongly recommended. Among their suggestions are the following:

1. Gather comprehensive location information at the outset from participants, friends, relatives, and any available records.
2. Establish formal and informal informational relationships with other public and private agencies with whom consumers may come in contact.
3. Create a public project identity. This is to convey to the community at large, and consumers and their advocates, that information about the long-term well-being of consumers is a "big deal" and important.
4. Above and beyond all else, the importance of tracking consumers must be emphasized to project staff. Often, a lot of tedious and repetitious detective work is required to locate and contact consumers after some period of time. The importance of this effort must be conveyed to the staff.
5. The simplest and cheapest tracking methods should be used first (e.g., city and county telephone directories).
6. Make involvement of the consumer in the evaluation convenient and rewarding, including possible financial inducements if possible.
7. Expend the greatest tracking efforts during the initial follow-up periods.
8. Tracking strategies and logistics must be customized for each individual evaluation project and for each participant (Ribisl et al., 1996).

THE "NUTS AND BOLTS" OF DATA COLLECTION

After the above array of issues have been processed and the evaluation planning decisions made, implementation planning must occur. The first task is a thorough orientation of staff members, at all levels, managerial through provider and support staff, about the purpose, importance, and logistics of the evaluation. The importance of a high rate of consumer participation, in particular, must be emphasized. There will always be some staff members who consider outcome evaluation foolish, irrelevant, and a waste of time. These individuals need special attention. If they cannot be convinced of the financial and survival value of outcome evaluation, they may be persuaded by the quality assurance aspects of feedback about consumers' adjustment and functioning. A last resort is informing such staff that support of the project is a job expectation. Unconvinced staff members can overtly or indirectly undermine the project if their cooperation is not elicited. A worthwhile strategy early in the project is to monitor consumer participation rates; high refusal rates may suggest lack of staff support of the project to consumers.

I experienced an example of the consequences of not fully informing *all* staff about the importance of the evaluation process during an initial implementation of outcome evaluation in a community mental health center outpatient service. The executive director actively supported the process, outpatient team leaders bought into the process, and the team leaders accepted responsibility for initial consumer-participation rates. However, 3 months later, completion rates of the admission administration of the evaluation instrument were still lingering around 50%. Investigation revealed that the intake secretary, who was responsible for assisting consumers with the initial paperwork and who was to administer the initial self-report assessment form, was not aware of the organization's commitment nor of the importance of high participation rates. She was, in fact, saying to the consumers, "Here is a form for you to fill out, but you don't really have to if you don't want to"; her nonverbal communication also indicated that completion of the form was not important. Several people had neglected to tell her that the assessments and high participation rates were important. A serious conversation with the secretary remedied the situation, and admission completion rates soon rose to over 90%.

The next matter to be dealt with is obtaining *consumers' informed consent.* There may be situations where provider organizations have incorporated outcome assessment and monitoring procedures into their normal operations to such an extent and for such a period of time that data collection can be legitimately considered a routine administrative and/or clinical process rather than as "research." In such situations "informed consent" may be less of an issue than in research settings. Although consumers have the legal right to refuse participation in all aspects of their relationship with the provider organization, just as they have the right to refuse treatment, the administrative waiving of obtaining informed consent should be legally reviewed.

In most service delivery settings at this time, however, the request to provide outcome evaluation information will be sufficiently novel that it must be considered research from a practical standpoint. The paradox here, of course, is that it is highly unlikely that requested outcome information will be any more sensitive than or qualitatively different from information elicited and discussed in the course of standard clinical practice. The consumer, however, must be informed that he is being asked to do something different or unusual, its purpose,

the risks or benefits involved, that he or she has the right to refuse to participate without jeopardizing his or her right to service, and his or her signed consent must be obtained.

There is a delicate strategic matter here that requires careful consideration.
As indicated earlier, it is important that a high proportion of consumers agree
to participate and provide outcome information; however, they also have the
right to know that they can refuse to participate. The sensitive balancing of
these two issues in presenting informed consent to consumers can make or
break the usefulness of the evaluation product. Nothing is required that is intrinsically beyond the capabilities of appropriate support staff, such as admission or intake secretaries. What is required is a mature attitude, sensitivity, and
interpersonal skills that allow the staff person to simultaneously convey to consumers that, although they have the right not to participate, their participation
is important to the organization and to future consumers. Thus, the selection of
a person with these attributes, and who is comfortable with and accepting of
the purposes of outcome evaluation, is extremely important. After the process
is begun, it is prudent to monitor consent rates for a month or two. If refusal
rates exceed 15–20%, the manner in which informed consent is being presented to consumers should be reexamined.

The next and perhaps central aspect of implementation is who is going to
actually collect the evaluation data. The three most common categories of data
collectors are clinical provider staff, organizational support staff, such as receptionists and intake secretaries, and independent or external interviewers.

From the provider organization's standpoint, perhaps the logistically simplest procedure, though potentially the most expensive, is hiring or arranging
for independent interviewers. Presumably the interviewers will have been selected because of requisite interpersonal skills, prior experience in interviewing, perhaps clinical research experience, and possibly because of training and
experience with the specific interview protocol or schedule to be used in the
outcome evaluation. If the interviewers are in fact adequately prepared, then
the main logistical issues are making interviewing space available and schedul-
ing or arranging for the interviewers and the participating consumers to get
together.

Self-administering questionnaires or scales are probably the next logistically
simplest approach. Because of their standardized format, administration of
such instruments generally does not require professional training, and they are
generally within the capabilities of mature support staff with good interpersonal skills. Intake secretaries, technicians, and receptionists can handle this
task, given some orientation and instruction. Such instructions include informing consumers that the questionnaire is part of the organization's efforts to
evaluate services, or to help see how participants are getting along. Although
clerical staff may be given permission to define questionnaire words that con-

sumers do not understand, emphasis must be given to their not providing or implying answers to the questions. A professional but neutral manner in relation to the scales is preferred. Good training and orientation procedures include demonstrating or role playing the process by the evaluator or a clinical staff person. Also useful is observing the support staff administering the instrument a few times. Persons administering these instruments should be counseled that some consumers will become anxious, and they should be prepared to reassure consumers that there are no right or wrong answers and to simply do the best they can. Consumers should be encouraged to respond to all the items if at all possible. They should also be alerted to being sensitive to consumers who cannot read or have difficulty reading. Such persons should be excused from completing the questionnaire (and the cohort). Once the routine has been established, administering such questionnaires to a consumer will usually take less than a minute of the support person's time. Although little time is required, support staff time is cheaper than professional provider time.

Probably the most psychologically burdensome approach for the organization is having professional clinical staff provide the outcome data (at admission and at later points). Again, most commonly used rating scales usually require only 2–3 minutes to complete. However, clinicians are already burdened with a great deal of paperwork, and providing outcome ratings is likely to be perceived as more bureaucratic busywork that interferes with their clinical work. The managerial task here is to be supportive and sympathetic while emphasizing that the data are important and may have important ramifications for the organization as a whole. If change data are to be reported back to clinicians periodically, and this is a good practice, the feedback and quality improvement aspects of the outcome evaluation can be emphasized.

Because of the difficulty standardizing rater interpretation and application of rating items, the use of clinician ratings as outcome measures is less straightforward than other methods. Unless the rating instrument has unusually specific and concrete definitions of the various rating points, such as the Hamilton Rating Scale for Depression (Hamilton, 1960), different raters are likely to place different meanings on the same rating scale points. Thus, it is desirable to have the raters go through the exercise of two or more clinicians rating the same client, or a videotape of a consumer be assessed (some such tapes are commercially available for purchase as training tools), and then reconciling their rating differences through discussion. Repeating this process will lead the clinicians to arrive at a general common interpretation of the different points on the scale. Because the meaning of the scale points tends to decay or "drift" over time, it is also desirable to periodically repeat this check on inter-rater agreement. This process of having clinicians discuss rating differences also helps identify and deal with clinician carelessness resulting from resentment of the procedure.

The final set of "nuts and bolts" have to do with data management. The first of these is assigning responsibility to a support staff person for monitoring completed data forms received vis-à-vis all eligible consumers (e.g., all new admissions). This person should also have the responsiblity of maintaining a calendar or tickler file indicating when individual consumers are due for a repeat assessment and then informing data collection or raters when these assessments are due. Someone in the management structure should have overall responsibility for the evaluation project. The monitoring support staff should report completion rates to the project manager who should have authority to intervene if problems develop in getting consumer consents or in data collection.

After the data forms have been logged into this monitoring list, the scales included in the forms must be scored by a clerical level person, and scores then entered into a computer or on data compilation sheets. Whether or not a computer is used for storing and analyzing the data may depend on the number of consumers in the evaluation cohort. With a large number (i.e., 60 or more), a computer will be useful. If the program is small (i.e., 20 or fewer consumers), simply recording the data on paper may be sufficient. The exception to the latter is if data on a large number of variables are being collected, and/or on numerous occasions. In this instance, use of a computer to analyze the data may be desirable in spite of a relatively small cohort. Most provider organizations will have someone on the staff who is computer literate and has had some experience using a computer to calculate simple statistics, such as averages, percentages, and t- tests. For example, all Ph.D. psychologists, or M.B.A.s, will have had at least rudimentary statistical and computer training. Relatively inexpensive basic statistical software is available if such is not already part of the management information system. If such a person is not available among staff, someone might be borrowed from another agency, a local college or university, or from a large local business or industry.

In summary, a number of issues central to decision making about and the planning of outcome evaluations have been discussed. Examples of outcome measures and comparison strategies for three groups of consumers varying in severity of distress, resources, and levels of functioning were presented. Although the importance of evaluating the immediate effects of treatment was pointed out, both the great importance and the difficulty of conducting follow-up evaluations were emphasized. Some practical suggestions for setting up the logistics of data collection and management are included.

REFERENCES

Cohen, S., & Williamson, G. (1988). Perceived stress in a probability sample of the United States. In S. Oskamp & S. Spacapan (Eds.), *The social psychology of health: Claremont symposium on applied psychology* (pp. 31–68). Newbury Park, CA: Sage.

Derogatis, L. R., & Spencer, P. M. (1982). *Administration and procedures: BSI Manual-I.* Riderwood, MD: Clinical Psychometric Research.

Dupuy, H. J. (1977). *A concurrent validational study of the NCHS General Well-being Schedule* (DHEW Publication No. HRA 78-1347). Hyattsville, MD: National Center for Health Statistics, U.S. Department of Health, Education, and Welfare.

Ellsworth, R. B. (1975). Consumer feedback in measuring the effectiveness of mental health programs. In M. Guttentay & E. L. Struennig (Eds.), *Handbook of evaluation research* (Vol. 2, pp. 239–274). Beverly Hills, CA: Sage.

Hamilton, M. A. (1960). A rating scale for depression. *Journal of Neurological and Neurosurgical Psychiatry, 25,* 56–62.

Kramer, H. B., Massey, O. T., & Pokorny, L. J. (1990). Development and validation of a level-of-care instrument for predicting residential placement. *Hospital and Community Psychiatry, 41,* 407–412.

Lehman, A., Kernan, E., & Postrado, L. (no date). *Toolkit for evaluating quality of life for persons with severe mental illness.* Baltimore: Center for Mental Health Services Research, University of Maryland School of Medicine.

Moos, R. H., & Moos, B. S. (1981). *Family Environment Scale manual.* Palo Alto, CA: Consulting Psycholgists Press.

O'Sullivan, M., & Speer, D. (1995). *The supported housing program, Broward County Elderly Services, Ft. Lauderdale, FL: Evaluation final report.* Tampa, FL: de la Parte Florida Mental Health Institute.

Overall, J. E., & Gorham, D. R. (1962). The Brief Psychiatric Rating Scale. *Psychological Reports, 10,* 799–812.

Peters, R. A., Kearns, W. D., Murrin, M. R., Dolente, A. S., & May, R. L. (1993). Examining the effectiveness of in-jail substance abuse treatment. *Journal of Offender Rehabilitation, 19,* 1–39.

Procidano, M. E., & Heller, K. (1983). Measures of perceived social support from friends and from family: Three validation studies. *American Journal of Community Psychology, 11,* 1–24.

Ribisl, K. M., Walton, M. A., Mowbray, C. T., Luke, D. A., Davidson, W. S., & Bootsmiller, B. J. (1996). Minimizing participant attrition in panel studies through the use of effective retention and tracking strategies: Review and recommendations. *Evaluation and Program Planning, 19,* 1–25.

Riggio, R. E. (1986). Assessment of basic social skills. *Journal of Personality and Social Psychology, 51,* 649–660.

Smith, V. L. (1996). Symptom Checklist-90-Revised (SCL-90-R) and the Brief Symptom Inventory (BSI). In L. I. Sederer & B. Dickey (Eds.), *Outcome assessment in clinical practice* (pp. 89–91). Baltimore: Williams & Wilkins.

Speer, D.C. (1978, August-September). *Effects of executive policy on client consent and participation rates, and exemplifying outcome results.* Paper presented at the 86th Annual Convention of the American Psychological Association, Toronto, Canada.

Speer, D. C., & Newman, F. L. (1996). Mental health services outcome evaluation. *Clinical Psychology: Science and Practice, 3,* 105–129.

Sperry, L., Brill, P. L., Howard, K. I., & Grisson, G. R. (1996). *Treatment outcomes in psychotherapy and psychiatric interventions.* New York: Brunner/Mazel.

CHAPTER 8

In Conclusion, Shouldn't Everybody Evaluate Outcomes? (and Other Loose Ends)

NOT NECESSARILY

In principle, I believe that all mental health service delivery organizations should be concerned about and attempt to assess their consumers' outcomes in some way. One school of thought about mental health service management is that the effect of services on consumers is the "bottom line." In business and industry, profit is the bottom line. Twenty years ago the American automobile industry learned that the number of units produced, alone, was insufficient to be competitive and to produce an acceptable level of profit. Similarly, the number of consumers seen, the number of units of service delivered, and cost per unit of service are no longer acceptable indices of the effectiveness of mental health service delivery organizations. In this framework, outcome assessment and monitoring could be viewed as basic management and governance functions.

Dr. Ronald Manderscheid, Chief, Survey and Analysis Branch, Substance Abuse and Mental Health Services Administration, recently stated that healthcare reform is rapidly moving toward viewing services in terms of outcomes as commodities. Consumers are increasingly demanding proof that services work. Manderscheid views outcome data as input into the service management system. He predicted that within 10 years providers would be paid on the basis of outcomes rather than on the basis of services provided (Manderscheid, 1996).

To be practical, not everybody should evaluate outcomes. There are a number of issues that must be dealt with in order for outcome evaluation procedures to be worth the effort, hassle, and cost, and not to yield misleading results. However, providers who do not start moving toward outcome evaluation appear to be doing so at their own peril.

ORGANIZATIONAL COMMITMENT

There have been instances when significant and important evaluation and research projects have been initiated informally and "on a shoestring" by line provider staff. Such efforts have usually been launched by questions of interest to clinical staff. Unfortunately, even though the results of such studies may find their way into professional journals, they usually do not find their way to the desks of policy and decision makers. There is usually little, if any, impact on the mental health service system.

As indicated earlier, if outcome evaluation findings are to have significant effects on the mental health treatment and care that consumers receive, people higher in the "power hierarchy" than provider line staff must be involved in the priority-setting and decision-making process. At a minimum, there must be a strong governance and management commitment to outcome assessment and the use of the findings. Half-hearted, lukewarm, or passive participation in the planning and implementation of outcome evaluation usually results in incomplete data, collected haphazardly and yielding data that are difficult if not impossible to interpret. Even though there may be interest at middle and line staff levels of the organization, without firm commitment "at the top" outcome evaluation processes have a consistent tendency to wind up at the bottom of the organization's functional priority list. As staff become aware of managerial indifference, this will affect their own commitment to data collection and supporting the process to consumers.

Ideally, top management, supported by the governing body, should "believe" in the importance and value of outcome evaluation in order for it to be done well and to produce usable findings. Obviously, the extent to which management commits and buys into outcome evaluation will determine the extent to which the findings will be used to make service delivery adjustments in the interest of better care for consumers. In the absence of at least moderately strong managerial commitment, it may be that outcome evaluation should not be attempted.

FUNDING SOURCES

It is difficult to imagine, in the late 1990s, that funding sources would not see the importance of and support outcome evaluation at the local level. Their endorsement, encouragement, and support of the evaluation processes can be of considerable value in conveying to service provider staff and the public that determining the effectiveness of services is important. There have been times in the past when program and budget reviewers from state mental health funding entities would skeptically question the appropriateness of program evaluation "studies" conducted by service-providing organizations. The assumption was that these were "research" activities and were more appropriate to academic settings.

Funding sources can lend support to local evaluation activities by publicly sanctioning, endorsing, and funding them. This can be done through media interviews, news releases, presentations to consumer advocacy groups and medical organizations, and talks at annual and public meetings and state conferences. Supporting outcome evaluation to legislative bodies, committees, and legislative staffs are also important. The goal of such support and public information is to convey to consumers and the public the importance of evaluating service effectiveness and that their help, assistance, and participation are needed. The more the public can be educated to view outcome evaluation as a natural, normal, and necessary part of managing and providing mental health services, the more successful outcome evaluation is likely to be. Although sanction and endorsement by public funding sources are probably not absolute necessities for conducting evaluation, they can be of considerable help on the public relations and public education dimensions of the evaluation enterprise.

In a somewhat different vein, funding sources that believe in the importance of and are seeking outcome information, whether they be private sector, managed care entities, or public sector, have at least two general obligations. The first, and perhaps easier, is the responsibility to think through specifically what kinds of outcome dimensions are important to the organization (i.e., distress reduction, improved family relationships, employment, inpatient days, etc.). Ideally, this would be done in collaboration with the provider system and personnel so that common interests and concerns could be negotiated and identified. The second obligation, particularly if the funding source is the impetus for outcome evaluation, is to participate in planning the methodology and planning the funding of the resultant evaluation.

Given the charged atmosphere of health-care cost containment, the timing of discussions of funding outcome evaluation is not good. The mental health industry is between the proverbial "rock" of needing service effectiveness information and the "hard place" of decreasing resources. Perhaps the hidden benefit of this situation is the necessity for funders, providers, and evaluators together to make the hard trade-off decisions regarding kinds of outcome information and their sources, their respective limitations, and the costs involved. For example, independent inteviewers may provide the most robust and independent sources of outcome data, but they may also be costly in terms of training and time spent interviewing. A compromise might be the temporary reassignment of salaried providers for evaluation interviewing, assuming the sanction of the funding source. Salaried current staff will likely be less expensive than contracted external private practice interviewers. The process will likely be a continuous series of trade-offs. The situation that all should strive to avoid is the untenable mandating of unfunded evaluation without giving thought and discussion to the effects on the quality of the resulting data (e.g., Speer, O'Sullivan and Lester, 1996).

CONSUMERS WHO DO NOT GET BETTER

As mentioned earlier, outcome evaluation is not completely without stress and risk. Admittedly there are not yet consensually accepted criteria for effective services. However, the evolving methodology for determining the significance of individual consumer change is producing findings that may be potentially disquieting to the mental health service industry. For example, a small group of studies of change among outpatients using Jacobson's approach for determing change (Chapter 3) have consistently found statistically reliable improvement among 50–60% of outpatients, that about 35–40% appear unchanged, and that 5–10% appear significantly worse at the end of treatment than at admission (e.g., Jacobson et al., 1984; Jacobson, Wilson, & Tupper, 1988; Speer & Greenbaum, 1995).

More sophisticated methods have produced even more unsettling findings. Jacobson and Truax (1991) reported that only 33% of their treated marital couples both improved significantly *and* moved from the dysfunctional range at admission to the normal range at the end of treatment. Using more stringent criteria for "recovery," the National Institute of Mental Health Treatment of Depression Collaborative Research Program found that only 24% of consumers with major depression, treated as outpatients with 18 sessions of service, were relatively free of symptoms at the end of treatment *and* at 18 months posttreatment (Elkin, 1994). There is a growing body of outcome literature pertaining to intensive case management (ICM) for persistently and severely mentally ill adults. These studies indicate that ICM is generally very effective in helping consumers with mental illness stay out of hospitals and reducing their lengths of stay when they do go into psychiatric inpatient care. However, these studies also suggest that ICM does little to reduce consumer distress and symptoms, and little to enhance daily functioning (Speer & Newman, 1996). O'Sullivan and Speer (1995) found that half of older adult persistently and severely mentally ill consumers reported dysfunctional levels of stress on one or more occasions over a 2-year period.

The upshot is that not all consumers get better, and some actually become worse. This, of course, is something that clinical providers have known for a long time, but nobody has wanted to face or talk about. As we move increasingly toward going public with our outcome findings, questions will arise about those consumers who do not improve noticeably or who become worse. Responding to such questions is where outcome evaluation can become sticky and stressful. However, given the mystique that has surrounded mental health and psychiatric services for decades, I believe that publicly sharing that such services are not perfect and that we cannot help everyone will in the long run enhance the credibility of the mental health industry. It will be useful to keep in mind, in spite of the above, that mental health services are as effective as, and in some instances more effective than, medical treatments for medical conditions (Lipsey & Wilson, 1993).

On the one hand, provider organizations (and perhaps funding sources) who are not conceptually prepared to dialogue with the public and policy makers about the facts that not all consumers improve demonstrably, and that a few become worse, should perhaps delay their participation in outcome evaluation. Confronting these phenomena are almost inevitable consequences of service outcome evaluation. On the other hand, outcome evaluation forces providers to think through the various consumer characteristics and service and program variables that may be involved in the failure of some consumers to change and others to seemingly deteriorate. These are integral components of service quality and effectiveness improvement.

OUTCOMES MANAGEMENT AND QUALITY IMPROVEMENT

Sperry, Brill, Howard, and Grissom (1996) have recently pointed out that there are at least two important uses of outcome findings. The first is the auditing or accounting function of tabulating relative "successes and failures" by program for policy makers, funding sources, governing bodies, and upper management. The second function is incorporation of outcome assessment into quality monitoring, assurance, and improvement processes. This might best be accomplished by providing individual providers, team managers, and the quality assurance committee with the outcome- monitoring data by individual consumers. This will provide clinical staff with feedback about their consumers, and will allow everyone to be aware of consumers who appear not to be progressing or who seem to be getting worse. Discussions of such consumers can lead to decisions to change treatment approaches, different service strategies, and perhaps a change of specific providers. The accumulation of insights gained through such monitoring and clinical management discussions can also potentially lead to programmatic and treatment management changes that enhance the overall quality and effectiveness of services.

The incorporation of outcome data into feedback and quality assurance processes has the additional benefit of making the evaluation process more real to clinical staff and demonstrating the quality improvement effects of outcome evaluation. This in turn may well lead to greater staff support and cooperation in implementation of the evaluation process. I have had the experience of receiving Symptom Checklist-90 (SCL-90) feedback data from consumers during outpatient treatment. Particularly useful were self-report symptom data that were discrepant with my perception of the consumers and the treatment process.

IN CONCLUSION

The mental health field is currently a turbulent mix of cost and utilization reduction forces, aggressive management, questions about service effectiveness, proprietary and public interests, potential opportunities, and professional and public outcries about the apparent erosion of quality care and seeming lack of concern about the care consumers receive. There is much agitation, distrust, apprehension, and resentment in the various constituent sectors of the industry. Increasingly noisy concerns about quality and effectiveness of services, and potential backlash against the current narrow focus of mental health management and funders on cost containment may well provide opportunities for improved services and care in the future. The vehicles for transforming these concerns and opportunities into improvements will be outcome assessment, identification of groups of consumers who do not respond to current interventions or who have high relapse rates, seeking answers to why they do not respond, service modification, and increasing use of outcome management and continuous quality improvement mechanisms. When the wave of concern about quality of care peaks, we must be positioned to vigorously address more sophisticated outcome and effectiveness issues.

Although mental health services will undoubtedly continue to be *managed* to a much greater extent than ever before, it is unlikely that the methods and technology in vogue today will be operant 10 years from now. Service outcomes and outcome management will become much more basic than is presently the case. Our influence on the future form of service delivery and management technology will be a function of tomorrow's innovations and effectiveness evaluations.

Because services and evaluation research have been late in arriving on the service delivery scene, the mental health service field is in a "catch-up" mode. New outcome evaluation methods are rapidly being developed, and there is a flurry of testing and trying out of new and old public-domain and proprietary methods. Proprietary technology is being marketed. Technology and sophistication are increasing. Although significant advances are being made, the "silver bullet" of efficient, valid, and credible outcome methodology has not yet been developed. The reader is cautioned that all currently available methods have flaws and shortcomings. Outcome evaluation methods and systems should not be set in concrete, but rather tested, evaluated, modified, and tested again.

As stated at the beginning, it is imperative that mental health provider organizations more actively and extensively participate in the development and field testing of methods and systems. Apart from the development and use of outcome evaluation methods, there are other important questions demanding attention. For example, why do such high proportions of consumers drop out of ambulatory services? Why do consumers stop taking their medications? Are there palatable and cost-efficient alternatives? How much psychosocial intervention and medication are needed to prevent relapse? These are tense and stressful but exciting times that provide much opportunity for development of new ways of providing improved care for troubled people.

REFERENCES

Elkin, I. (1994). The NIMH treatment of depression collaborative research program: Where we began and where we are. In A. E. Bergin & S. L. Garfield (Eds.), *Handbook of psychotherapy and behavior change* (pp. 114–139). New York: John Wiley & Sons.

Jacobson, N. S., Follette, W. C., Revenstorf, D., Baucom, D. H., Hohlweg, K., & Margolin, D. (1984). Variability in outcome and clinical significance of behavioral marital therapy: A reanalysis of outcome data. *Journal of Consulting and Clinical Psychology, 53*, 497–504.

Jacobson, N. S., & Truax, P. (1991). Clinical significance: A statistical approach to defining meaningful change in psychotherapy research. *Journal of Consulting and Clinical Psychology, 59*, 12–19.

Jacobson, N. S., Wilson, L., & Tupper, C. (1988). The clinical significance of treatment gains resulting from exposure-based interventions for agoraphobia: A reanalysis of outcome data. *Behavioral Therapy, 19*, 539–552.

Lipsey, M. W., & Wilson, D. B. (1993). The efficacy of psychological, educational, and behavioral treatment: Confirmation from meta-analysis. *American Psychologst, 48*, 1181–1209.

Manderscheid, R. (1996, November). *Improving the quality of managed care: What providers can do.* Paper presented at the Third Annual Florida Conference on Behavioral Healthcare Evaluation. Orlando, FL.

O'Sullivan, M., & Speer, D. (1995). *The supported housing program, Broward County Elderly Services, Ft. Lauderdale, FL: Evaluation final report.* Tampa, FL: de la Parte Florida Mental Health Institute.

Speer, D. C., & Greenbaum, P. E. (1995). Five methods for computing significant individual client change and improvement rates: Support for an individual growth curve approach. *Journal of Consulting and Clinical Psychology, 63*, 1044–1048.

Speer, D. C., & Newman, F. L. (1996). Mental health services outcome evaluation. *Clinical Psychology: Science and Practice, 3,* 105–129.

Speer, D. C., O'Sullivan, M. J., & Lester, W. A. (1996). Impact of mental health services in nursing homes: The clinicians' perspective. *Journal of Clinical Geropsychology, 2,* 83–92.

Sperry, L., Brill, P. L., Howard, K. I., & Grissom, G. R. (1996). *Treatment outcomes in psychotherapy and psychaitric interventions.* New York: Brunner/Mazel.

INDEX